FLORENCE NIGHTINGALE

FLORENCE NIGHTINGALE

BY

LAURA E. RICHARDS

YESTERDAY'S CLASSICS

CHAPEL HILL, NORTH CAROLINA

This edition, first published in 2007 by Yesterday's Classics, an imprint of Yesterday's Classics, LLC, is an unabridged republication of the work originally published by D. Appleton and Company in 1909. For the complete listing of the books that are published by Yesterday's Classics, please visit www.yesterdaysclassics.com. Yesterday's Classics is the publishing arm of the Baldwin Online Children's Literature Project which presents the complete text of hundreds of classic books for children at www.mainlesson.com.

ISBN-10: 1-59915-220-7
ISBN-13: 978-1-59915-220-2

Yesterday's Classics, LLC
PO Box 3418
Chapel Hill, NC 27515

TO

THE SISTER ELEANOR

OF THE SISTERHOOD OF SAINT MARY

HERSELF THROUGH MANY LONG YEARS
A DEVOTED WORKER FOR THE POOR,
THE SICK, AND THE SORROWFUL, THIS
BRIEF RECORD OF AN HEROIC LIFE IS
AFFECTIONATELY DEDICATED

For the material used in this little book I am chiefly indebted to Sarah A. Tooley's "Life of Florence Nightingale," and to Kinglake's "Invasion of the Crimea."

CONTENTS

CONTENTS

CHAPTER I

HOW FLORENCE GOT HER NAME

ONE evening, some time after the great Crimean War of 1854–55, a company of military and naval officers met at dinner in London. They were talking over the war, as soldiers and sailors love to do, and somebody said: "Who, of all the workers in the Crimea, will be longest remembered?"

Each guest was asked to give his opinion on this point, and each one wrote a name on a slip of paper. There were many slips, but when they came to be examined there was only one name, for every single man had written "Florence Nightingale."

Every English boy and girl knows the beautiful story of Miss Nightingale's life. Indeed, hers is perhaps the best-loved name in England since good Queen Victoria died. It will be a great pleasure to me to tell this story to our own boys and girls in this country;

1

and it shall begin, as all proper stories do, at the beginning.

Her father was named William Nightingale. He was an English gentleman, and in the year 1820 was living in Italy with his wife. Their first child was born in Naples, and they named her Parthenope, that being the ancient name of Naples; two years later, when they were living in Florence, another little girl came to them, and they decided to name her also after the city of her birth.

When Florence was still a very little child her parents came back to England to live, bringing the two children with them. First they went to a house called Lea Hall, in Derbyshire. It was an old, old house of gray stone, standing on a hill, in meadows full of buttercups and clover. All about were blossoming hedgerows full of wild roses, and great elder-bushes heavy with white blossoms; and on the hillside below it lies the quaint old village of Lea with its curious little stone houses.

Lea Hall is a farmhouse now, but it still has its old flag-paved hall and its noble staircase of oak with twisted balustrade, and broad solid steps where little Florence and her sister "Parthe" used to play and creep and tumble. There was another place near by where they loved even better to play; that was the ancient house of Dethick. I ought rather to say the ancient kitchen, for little else remained of the once stately mansion. The rest of the house was comparatively new, but the great kitchen was (and no doubt is) much as it was in the days of Queen Elizabeth.

Imagine a great room with heavy timbered roof, ponderous oaken doors, and huge open fireplace over which hung the ancient roasting jack. In the ceiling was a little trap-door, which looked as if it might open on the roof; but in truth it was the entrance to a chamber hidden away under the roof, a good-sized room, big enough for several persons to hide in.

Florence and her sister loved to imagine the scenes that had taken place in that old kitchen; strange and thrilling, perhaps terrible scenes; they knew the story of Dethick, and now you shall hear it too.

In that old time which Tennyson calls "the spacious days of great Elizabeth," Dethick belonged to a noble family named Babington. It was a fine house then. The oaken door of the old kitchen opened on long corridors and passages, which in turn led to stately halls and noble galleries. There were turrets and balconies overlooking beautiful gardens; and on the stone terraces gay lords and ladies used to walk and laugh and make merry, and little children run and play and dance, and life go on very much as it does now, with work and play, love and laughter and tears.

One of the gay people who used to walk there was Anthony Babington. He was a gallant young gentleman, an ardent Catholic, and devoted to the cause of the beautiful and unfortunate Mary Queen of Scots.

Though ardent and devoted, Babington was a weak and foolish young man. He fell under the influence of a certain Ballard, an artful and designing person who had resolved to bring about the death of the great English Queen, and was induced by him to form

3

the plot which is known in history as Babington's Conspiracy; so he was brought to ruin and death.

In the year 1586 Queen Mary was imprisoned at Wingfield Manor, a country house only a few miles distant from Dethick. The conspirators gathered other Catholic noblemen about them, and planned to release Queen Mary and set her once more on the throne.

They used to meet at Dethick, where, it is said, there is a secret passage underground leading to Wingfield Manor. Perhaps—who knows?—they may have sat in the kitchen, gathering about the great fireplace for warmth; the lights out, for fear of spies, only the firelight gleaming here and there, lighting up the dark corners and the eager, intent faces. And when the plot was discovered, and Queen Elizabeth's soldiers were searching the country round for the young conspirators, riding hither and thither along the pleasant country lanes and thrusting their sabres in among the blossoming hedgerows, it was here at Dethick that they sought for Anthony Babington. They did not find him, for he was in hiding elsewhere, but one of his companions was actually discovered and arrested there.

Perhaps—again, who knows?—this man may have been hiding in the secret chamber above the trap-door. One can fancy the pursuers rushing in, flinging open cupboards and presses, in search for their prey; and finding no one, gathering baffled around the fireplace. Then one, chancing to glance up, catches sight of the trap-door in the ceiling. "Ha! lads, look up! the rascal may be hiding yonder! Up with you, you tall fellow!" Then a piling up of benches, one man mounting on another's shoulders—the door forced open, the young nobleman seized and overpowered, and brought down to be carried off to London for trial.

Anthony Babington and his companions were executed for high treason, and Queen Mary, who was convicted of approving the plot, was put to death soon after.

All this Florence Nightingale and her sister knew, and they never tired of "playing suppose" in old Dethick kitchen, and living over again in fancy the romantic time long past. And on Sundays the two children went with their parents to old Dethick church, and sat where Anthony Babington used to sit, for in his days it was the private chapel of Dethick. It is a tiny church; fifty people would fill it to overflowing, but Florence and her sister might easily feel that the four bare walls held all the wild history of Elizabeth's reign.

Anthony Babington in doublet and hose, with velvet mantle, feathered cap, and sword by his side; little Florence Nightingale in round Leghorn hat and short petticoats. It is a long step between these two, yet they are the two most famous people who ever said their prayers in old Dethick church. The lad's brief and tragic story contrasts strangely with the long and beautiful story of Florence Nightingale, a story that has no end.

When Florence was between five and six years old, she left Lea Hall for a new home, Lea Hurst, about a mile distant. Here her father had built a beautiful house in the Elizabethan style, of stone, with pointed gables, mullioned windows and latticed panes. There was a tiny chapel on the site he chose, hundreds of years old, and this he built into the house, so that Lea Hurst, as well as Lea Hall and Dethick, joined hands with the old historic times. In this little chapel, by and by, we shall see Florence holding her Bible class. But I like still to think of her as a little rosy girl, running about the beautiful gardens of Lea Hurst, or playing house in the quaint old summerhouse with its pointed roof of thatch. Perhaps she brought her dolls here; but the dolls must wait for another chapter.

Soon after moving to Lea Hurst, the Nightingales bought still another country seat, Embley Park, in Hampshire, a fine old mansion built in Queen Elizabeth's time, and at some distance from Lea Hurst.

After this the family used to spend the summer at Lea Hurst, and the winter at Embley. There were no railroads then in that neighborhood; the journey was sometimes made by stagecoach, sometimes in the Nightingales' own carriage.

Embley Park is one of the stately homes of England, with its lofty gables, terraces and shadowing trees; and all around it are sunny lawns, and gardens filled with every sweet and lovely flower.

Now you know a little of the three homes of Florence Nightingale, Lea Hall, Lea Hurst, and Embley Park; next you shall hear what kind of child she herself was.

CHAPTER II

LITTLE FLORENCE

ALL the boys, and very likely some of the girls, who have got as far as this second chapter, will glance down the page, and exclaim: *"Dolls!"* Then they will add whatever is their favorite expression of scorn, and perhaps make a motion to lay the book down.

Wait a moment, girls, and boys too! I advise you to read on, and see what came in this case of playing with dolls.

There were a good many thousands of boys in England at that time, in the Twenties and Thirties, who might have been badly off when the terrible Fifties came, if Florence Nightingale had not played with her dolls. Read on, and see for yourselves!

Florence Nightingale loved her dolls dearly, and took the greatest possible care of them; and yet they were always delicate and given to sudden and alarming illnesses. A doll never knew when she might be told that she was very ill, and undressed and put to bed, though she might but just have got on her new frock. Then Mamma Florence would wait upon her tenderly,

7

smoothing her pillow, bathing her forehead or rubbing her poor back, and bringing her all kinds of good things in the doll-house dishes. The doll might feel very much better the next day, and think it was time to get up and put on the new frock again; but she was very apt to have a relapse and go back to bed and gruel again, once at least, before she was allowed to recover entirely.

The truth is, Florence was born to be a nurse, and a sick doll was dearer to her than a strong and healthy one. So I fear her dolls would have been invalids most of the time if it had not been for Parthenope's little family, who often required their Aunt Florence's care. These dolls were very unlucky, or else their mamma was very careless; you can call it whichever you like. They were always tumbling down and breaking their heads, or losing arms and legs, or burning themselves at the nursery fire, or suffering from doll's consumption, that dreadful complaint otherwise known as loss of sawdust. When these things happened, Aunt Florence was called in as a matter of course; and she set the fractures, and salved the burns, and stopped the flow of sawdust, and proved herself in every way a most skillful nursery surgeon and physician.

So it was that unconsciously, and in play, Florence began her training for her life work. She was having lessons, of course; arithmetic, and all the other proper things. She and Parthe had a governess, and studied regularly, and had music and drawing lessons besides; and her father taught her to love English literature, and later opened to her the great doors marked *Latin* and *Greek*. Her mother, meantime, taught her all kinds of handiwork, and before she was twelve years old she could hemstitch, and seam and embroider. These things were all good, and very good; without them she could not have accomplished all she did; but in the years that were to come all the other learning was going to help that wonderful learning that began with nursing the sick dolls.

Soon she was to take another step in her profession. The little fingers grown so skillful by bandaging waxen and china arms and legs, were now to save a living, loving creature from death.

To every English child this story is a nursery tale. No doubt it is to many American children also, yet it is one that no one can ever tire of hearing, so I shall tell it again.

Much as Florence loved dolls, she loved animals better, and in her country homes she was surrounded by them. There was her dog, who hardly left her side when she was out of doors; there was her own pony on which she rode every day over dale and down; her sister's pony, too, and old Peggy, who was too old to work, and lived in a pleasant green paddock with nothing to do but amuse herself and crop grass all day long. Perhaps Peggy found this tiresome, for whenever she saw Florence at the gate she would toss her head and whinny and come trotting up to the gate. "Good morning, Peggy!" Florence would say. "Would you like an apple?"

"Hooonh!" Peggy would say. (Horses have no spelling books, and there is no exact rule as to how a whinny should be spelled. You may try any other way that looks to you more natural.)

"Then look for it!" Florence would reply. At this Peggy would sniff and snuff, and hunt round with her soft velvety nose till she found Florence's pocket, then delicately take out the apple and crunch it up, and whinny again, the second whinny meaning at once "Thank you!" and "More, please!" Horse language is a simple one compared to English, and has no grammar.

Well, one day Florence was riding her pony in company with her friend the vicar. This good man loved all living creatures, but there were few dearer to him than Florence Nightingale. They had the same tastes and feelings. Both loved to help and comfort all who were "in trouble, sorrow, need, sickness, or any other adversity." He had studied medicine before he became a clergyman, and so was able to tell her many things about the care of the sick and injured. Here was another teacher. I suppose everyone we know could teach us something good, if we were ready to learn.

As I said, Florence and the vicar were riding along on the green downs; and here I must stop again a moment to tell you what the downs are, for when I was a child I used to wonder. They are great rounded hills, covered with close, thick turf, like a velvet carpet. They spread in long smooth green billows, miles and miles of them, the slopes so gentle that it is delightful to drive or ride on them; only you must be careful not to go near the edge, where the green breaks off suddenly, and a white chalk cliff goes down, down, hundreds of feet, to the blue sea tossing and tumbling below. These are the white cliffs of England that you have so often read about.

Am I never going on with the story? Yes; have patience! there is plenty of time.

There were many sheep on the downs, and there was one special flock that Florence knew very well. It belonged to old Roger, a shepherd, who had often worked for her father. Roger and his good dog Cap were both friends of Florence's, and she was used to seeing them on the downs, the sheep in a more or less orderly compact flock, Cap guarding them and driving back any stragglers who went nibbling off toward the cliff edge.

But to-day there seemed no order anywhere. The sheep were scattered in twos and threes, straying hither and thither; and old Roger alone was trying to collect them, and apparently having a hard time of it.

The vicar saw his trouble, and rode up to him. "What is the matter, Roger?" he asked kindly. "Where is your dog?"

"The boys have been throwing stones at him, sir," replied the old man. "They have broken his leg, poor beast, and he will never be good for anything again. I shall have to take a bit of cord and put an end to his misery."

"Oh!" cried Florence, who had ridden up with the vicar. "Poor Cap! Are you sure his leg is broken, Roger?"

"Yes, Miss, it's broke sure enough. He hasn't set foot to the ground since, and no one can't go anigh him but me. Best put him out of his pain, I says."

"No! no!" cried Florence. "Not till we have tried to help him. Where is he?"

"He's in the cottage, Missy, but you can do nothing for him, you'll find. Poor Cap's days is over. Ah; he were a good dog. Do everything but speak, he could, and went as near to that as a dumb beast could. I'll never get another like him."

While the old man lamented, Florence was looking eagerly in the face of the clergyman. He met her look with a smile and nod.

"We will go and see!" he said; and off they rode, leaving Roger shaking his head and calling to the sheep.

They soon reached the cottage. The door was fastened, and when they tried to open it a furious barking was heard within. A little boy came from the next cottage, bringing the key, which Roger had left there. They entered, and there lay Cap on the brick floor, helpless and weak, but still barking as hard as he could at what he supposed to be intruders. When he saw Florence and the little boy he stopped barking, and wagged his tail feebly; then he crawled from under the table where he lay, dragged himself to Florence's feet and looked up pitifully in her face. She knelt down by him, and soothed and petted and talked to him, while the good clergyman examined the injured leg. It was dreadfully swollen, and every touch was painful; but Cap knew well enough that the hands that hurt were

12

trying to help him, and though he moaned and winced, he licked the hands and made no effort to draw the leg away.

"Is it broken?" asked Florence anxiously. "No," said the vicar. "No bones are broken. There's no reason why Cap should not recover; all he needs is care and nursing."

Florence quietly laid down her riding whip and tucked up her sleeves. "What shall I do first?" she said.

"Well," said the vicar, "I think a hot compress is the thing." Florence looked puzzled; the dolls had never had hot compresses. "What is it?" she asked.

"Just a cloth wrung out in boiling water and laid on, changing it as it cools. Very simple, you see, Nurse Florence! The first thing is to light the fire."

That was soon done, with the aid of the boy, who hovered about, interested, but ignorant of surgery. On went the kettle, and soon it was boiling merrily; but where were the cloths for the compresses? Florence looked all about the room, but could see nothing save Roger's clean smock frock which hung against the door.

"This will do!" she cried. "Mamma will give him another."

The vicar nodded approval. Quickly she tore the frock into strips of suitable width and length; bade the boy fill a basin from the kettle, and then kneeling down beside the wounded dog, Florence Nightingale for the first time gave "first aid to the wounded."

As the heat drew out the inflammation and pain, Cap looked up at the little helper, all his simple dog heart shining in his eyes; the look sank into the child's heart and deepened the tenderness already there. Another step, and a great one, was taken on the blessed road she was to travel.

Florence came again the next day to bandage the leg; Cap got entirely well, and tended sheep for many a year after that; and old Roger was very grateful, and Mrs. Nightingale gave him a new smock frock, and everyone was happy; and that is the end of the story.

CHAPTER III

THE SQUIRE'S DAUGHTER

IT soon became a recognized thing in Florence's own home and in all the neighborhood, that she was one of the Sisters of Mercy. Nothing was too small, no creature too humble to awaken her sympathy and tenderness. When the stable cat had kittens, Florence was the first to visit them, to fondle the tiny creatures and soothe their mother's angry fear. When she walked along the pleasant wood roads of Lea Hurst, the squirrels expected nuts as a matter of course, and could hardly wait for her to give them. When anyone in the village or farm fell ill, it was Florence who was looked for to cheer and comfort. Mrs. Nightingale was a most kind and charitable lady, and delighted in sending delicacies to the sick. It was Florence's happy privilege to carry them, and whether she walked or rode there was apt to be a basket on her arm or fastened to her saddlebow.

If you think hard, you can see—at least I can— just how it would be. Old Goody Brown's rheumatism, let us say, was very bad one morning. You children who read this know little about rheumatism. Very likely you think it rather a funny word, and that it is just a thing that old people have, and that they make a good deal of fuss about. If it were a toothache, now, you say, or colic—but the truth is, no pain is in any way pleasant. If a red-hot sword were run into your back you would not like it? Well, sometimes rheumatism is like that.

So old Goody Brown was suffering, and very cross, just as we might be; and nothing suited her, poor old soul; her tea was too hot, and her porridge too cold, and her pillow set askew, and—dear! dear! dear! she wished she was dead, so she did. Martha, her good patient daughter, was at her wits' ends.

"Send to the 'All'!" said poor old Goody. "Send for Miss Florence! She'll do something for me, I know."

So a barefoot boy would trudge up to the great house, and very soon a light, slight figure would come quickly along the village street and enter the cottage. A slender girl, quietly dressed, with perfect neatness and taste; brown hair smoothly parted, shining like satin; gray-blue eyes full of light and thoughtfulness; regular features, an oval face, cheeks faintly tinted with rose—this was Florence Nightingale.

I cannot tell you just what she had in the little basket on her arm, whether jelly or broth or chicken or oranges; there was sure to be something good beside the liniment and medicines to help the aching back and limbs. But the basket held the least of what she brought. At the very sound of her voice the fretful lines melted away from the poor old face. I cannot tell you—I wish I could—the words she said, this little Sister of Mercy, yet I can almost hear her speak, in that sweet, cordial voice whose range held no harsh note; can see her setting the pillow straight and smooth, making the little tray dainty and pretty with the posy she had brought, coaxing the old woman to eat, making her laugh over some story of her pets and their droll ways. Perhaps before leaving she would open the worn Bible or prayer book, and read a psalm; can you not see her sitting by the bedside, her pretty head bent over the book, her face full of tenderness and reverence? I am sure that when she went away there was peace and comfort in that cottage room, and that heartfelt blessings followed the "Angel Child" as she went on her homeward way. "She had a way with her," they said; and that meant more than volumes of praise.

The flowers that Florence used to carry were from her own garden, I like to think. Both at Lea Hurst and Embley, she and her sister had each her own little garden and gardening tools. Florence was a good gardener; indeed, I think she was a good everything that she tried to be, just because she tried. She dug, and sowed, and watered, pruned and tied up and did all the things a garden needs; and so her garden was full of flowers all summer long, giving delight to her and to every sick or lonely or sorrowful person for miles around.

As Florence and her sister grew older they became more and more helpful to their parents in the good works that they both loved to carry on. I have read a delightful account of the "feast day" of the village school-children, as it used to be given at Lea Hurst when Florence was a girl.

The children gathered together at the school-house, all in their best frocks and pinafores, and walked in procession up the street and through the fields to Lea Hurst. Each child carried a posy and a stick wreathed with flowers, and at the head of the procession marched a band of music, provided by the good squire. In the field below the garden tables were set, and here Mrs. Nightingale and her daughters, aided by the servants, served tea and buns and cakes, waiting on their little guests, and seeing that every child got all he wanted—or at least all that was good for him. Then when all had eaten and drunk their fill, the band struck up, and the boys and girls danced on the green to their hearts' content.

What did they dance? Polkas, perhaps, and the redowa, a pretty round dance with a good deal of stamping in it; and of course Sir Roger de Coverley, which is very like our Virginia Reel. (If you do not know about Sir Roger de Coverley himself, ask papa to tell you or read you about him, for he is one of the pleasantest persons you will ever know.)

Perhaps they sang, too; perhaps they sang the pretty old Maypole Song. Do you know it?

> Come lasses and lads, get leave of your dads,
> And away to the Maypole hie,
> For ev'ry fair has a sweetheart there,
> And the fiddler's standing by.
> For Willy shall dance with Jane,
> And Johnny has got his Joan,
> To trip it, trip it, trip it, trip it,
> Trip it up and down.

18

"You're out!" says Dick, "not I," says Nick,
" 'Twas the fiddler play'd it wrong."
" 'Tis true," says Hugh, and so says Sue,
And so says ev'ry one;
The fiddler then began
To play the tune again,
And ev'ry girl did trip it, trip it,
Trip it to the men.

Then when feast and dance and song were all over, it was time to re-form the procession and take up the homeward march. The two sisters, Florence and Parthe, had disappeared during the dancing; but now, as the procession passed along the terrace, there they were, standing behind a long table; a table at sight of which the children's eyes grew round and bright, for it was covered from end to end with presents. Such delightful presents! Books, and pretty boxes and baskets, thimble-cases and needle-books and pin-cushions; dolls, too, I am sure, for the little ones, and scrap-books, and—but you can fill up the list for yourself with everything you like best in the way of pretty, simple, useful gifts. I am quite sure that Florence would not have wished to give the children foolish or elaborate gimcracks, and that Mr. Nightingale would never have allowed it if she had; and I think it probable that many of the gifts were made by the two sisters and their kind and clever mother.

All about Lea Hurst, in many and many a pleasant cottage home, those little gifts are treasured to-day like the relics of some blessed saint; which indeed is just what they are. The saint is still living, and some of the children of the school feasts are living, too, and now in their age will show with pride and joy the gifts they received long ago from the hands of the beloved Miss Florence.

As Florence grew up to womanhood she found more and more work to do. There were mills and factories in the neighborhood of Lea Hurst; and in the hosiery mills, especially, hundreds of women and girls were employed, many of whom lived on the Nightingale estate.

She may have been seventeen or eighteen when she started her Bible class for the young women of the district, holding it in the tiny ancient chapel at Lea Hurst which I described in the first chapter. Gathering the girls around her, she would read a chapter from the Bible, and then give them her thoughts about it, and explain the difficult passages; then they would all sing together, her sweet, clear voice leading the hymns. Here is another memory very precious to the old women who were once those happy girls. They love to tell "how beautifully Miss Florence used to talk."

Long years after, when Miss Nightingale, spent with her noble labors, would come to Lea Hurst for a time of rest and refreshment, the daughters of these girls counted it a high privilege to gather on the lawn under her window and sing to her as she sat in the room above; and would go home proud and happy as queens if they had seen the saintly face smiling from the window.

Shall I try to show you Florence Nightingale at seventeen? Her face was little changed from that of the girl we saw in the cottage, cheering old Goody Brown. She still wore her hair brushed smoothly "Madonnawise" on either side her face; often, now, she wore a rose at the side, tucked in among the shining braids or coils. You would think her frocks very queer if you saw them today, but then they were extremely pretty; full skirts (no crinoline! that was to come later) and full sleeves, with broad flat collar of lace or embroidery. When she went to church or to make visits she wore a spencer, a kind of full plaited jacket with a belt, something like a Norfolk jacket—only different! and a Leghorn bonnet. You have seen pictures of the Leghorn bonnets of the Thirties and Forties; "coal-scuttles," some people called them, and they were something the shape of a scuttle. Some of them were enormous in size, and they look queer enough now in the pictures, or—if your grandmamma had a way of keeping things—in the "dress-up" trunk or cupboard in the attic. But people who were young in those days tell me that they were extremely becoming, and that a pretty face never looked prettier than when it peeped out from the depths of a huge straw "coal-scuttle."

When Florence rode on horseback, her habit was so long that it nearly touched the ground (that is, if she followed the fashion of the day, but I should not wonder a bit if she and her mother were too sensible!) and she wore a round, broad-brimmed hat with long ostrich plumes. I remember a picture of the Princess Royal (afterwards Empress Frederick of Germany), in a costume like this, which I thought one of the most beautiful things I ever saw, so I shall imagine Florence, on an afternoon ride with the squire, let us say, dressed in this way; but when scampering about on her pony, I trust, she wore a less cumbrous costume.

You will remember that the Nightingales spent the winter at Embley Park, in Hampshire. Here, too, Florence was busy in good and helpful work. At Christmas time she found her best pleasure in giving presents to young and old among the poor people about her, in getting up entertainments for the children, training them to sing, arranging treats for the old people in the poorhouse. On Christmas Eve the village carol singers would come and sing on the lawn; old English carols, that had been sung by generation after generation. Poor Anthony Babington over at Lea Hall may have listened on Christmas Eve to the same sweet old songs.

As Joseph was a-walking,
He heard an angel sing,
"This night shall be the birthnight
Of Christ our heavenly King.

"His birth-bed shall be neither
In housen nor in hall,
Nor in the place of paradise,
But in the oxen's stall.

"He neither shall be rocked
In silver nor in gold,
But in the wooden manger
That lieth in the mold.

"He neither shall be washen
With white wine nor with red,
But with the fair spring water
That on you shall be shed.

"He neither shall be clothed
In purple nor in pall,
But in the fair white linen
That usen babies all."

As Joseph was a-walking,
Thus did the angel sing,
And Mary's son at midnight
Was born to be our King.

Then be you glad, good people,
At this time of the year;
And light you up your candles,
For His star it shineth clear.

Then who so glad as Florence to call the singers in and bid them welcome and "Merry Christmas!" and aid in distributing the mince pies and silver coins which were always their due.

When Florence was fairly "grown up," other things came into her life, the gay and merry things that come to so many girls. Mr. Nightingale was a man of wealth and position, and liked his wife and daughters to have their share in the gayeties of the county. So there were many parties, at Embley and elsewhere, and Florence danced as gayly, I doubt not, as the other girls. She went to London, too, and she and her sister were presented to Queen Victoria, and had their share of the brilliant society of the time.

But much as she may have enjoyed all this for a time, still her heart was not in it, and she soon tired, I fancy, of dancing and dressing and visiting. Already her mind was turning to other things, already her clear eyes were looking forward to other ways of life, other methods of work.

CHAPTER IV

LOOKING OUT

TEP by step, and all unconsciously, Florence Nightingale had been training her hand and eye to follow the dictates of her keen mind and loving heart. Now, grown a young woman, she began to think seriously how she should apply this training. What should she do with her life? Should she go on like her friends, in the quiet pleasant ways of country life? The squire's daughter was busy enough, surely. Every hour of the day was full of useful, kindly work, of happy, healthy play; should she be content with this? Her heart told her that she was not content. In her friendly visiting among the sick poor she had seen much misery and suffering, far more than she and all the other kindly ladies could attempt to relieve. She felt that something more was needed; she began to look around to see what was being done in the larger world. It was about this time that she met Elizabeth Fry, the noble and beautiful friend of the prisoner. Mrs. Fry was then an elderly woman, with all the glory of her saintly life shining about her; Florence Nightingale an earnest and thoughtful girl of perhaps eighteen or twenty. It is pleasant to think of that meeting. I do not know what words passed between them, but I can almost see them together, the beautiful stately woman in her Quaker dress, the slender girl with her quiet face and earnest eyes; can almost hear the young voice, questioning, eager and ardent; the elder answering, grave and sedate, words full of weight and wisdom, of sweetness and tenderness. This interview was one of the great moments of Florence Nightingale's early life.

A little later than this, in 1843, she met another person whose words and counsel impressed her deeply; and of this meeting I can give you a clearer account, for that person was my own dear father, Dr. Samuel G. Howe. Some ten years before this my father had decided to devote his life to helping people who needed help. He had established a school for the blind in Boston; he had brought Laura Bridgman, the blind, deaf mute, out of her loneliness and taught her to read, write, and talk with her fingers; the first time this had ever been done with a person so afflicted. He had labored to help the prisoners and captives in the North, and the slaves in the South; in short he was what is called a *philanthropist*, that is, one who loves his fellowmen and tries to help them.

My father and mother were traveling in England soon after their marriage, and were invited by Mr. and Mrs. Nightingale to spend a few days at Embley Park. One morning Miss Nightingale (for so I must call her now that she is a woman) met my father in the garden and said to him:

"Dr. Howe, you have had much experience in the world of philanthropy; you are a medical man and a gentleman; now may I ask you to tell me, upon your word, whether it would be anything unsuitable or unbecoming to a young Englishwoman, if she should devote herself to works of charity, in hospitals and elsewhere, as the Catholic Sisters do?"

My father replied: "My dear Miss Florence, it would be unusual, and in England whatever is unusual is apt to be thought unsuitable; but I say to you, go forward, if you have a vocation for that way of life; act up to your aspiration, and you will find that there is never anything unbecoming or unladylike in doing your duty for the good of others. Choose your path, go on with it, wherever it may lead you, and God be with you!"

It was in this spirit that Miss Nightingale now began to train herself for her life work.

It is hard for you children of to-day to imagine what nursing was in the early part of the nineteenth century. To you a nurse means a trim, alert, cheerful person in spotless raiment, who knows just what to do when you are ill, and does it in the pleasantest possible manner; you are glad when she comes into the room, sorry when she leaves. But this pleasant person did not exist in those days, except in the guise of a Catholic Sister of Charity. The other nurses were for the most part coarse and ignorant women, often cruel, often intemperate. When you read "Martin Chuzzlewit" you will find out more about them than I can tell you. But "Martin Chuzzlewit" was not written when Miss Nightingale determined to find out the condition of nursing in England and on the Continent. She first spent some months in the London hospitals, and then visited those in Scotland and Ireland. She was horrified at what she found there; dirt and misery and needless suffering among the patients, drunkenness and ignorance and brutality among the nurses. Then she turned to the Continent and found a very different state of things. The hospitals were clean and cheerful, and the Sisters of Mercy in their white caps and aprons were as good and kind and capable as our trained nurses today.

Up to this time these good sisters had been the only trained nurses in Europe; but in Germany Miss Nightingale found a Protestant sisterhood which was working along the same lines, and in a more enlightened and modern way; these were the Deaconesses of Kaiserswerth, the pupils of Pastor Fliedner.

This good man—one of the best men, surely, that ever lived—was the son of a Lutheran minister. His father was poor, and Theodore had to work his way through college, but this he did cheerfully, for he loved work. He studied very hard and also gave lessons, sawed wood, blacked boots, and did other odd jobs. When his clothes began to wear out he sewed up the holes with white thread, all he had, and then inked it over. He loved children, and on the long tramps he used to take in vacation time he was always collecting songs and games, and teaching them to the children.

When he was twenty-two years old Theodore Fliedner became pastor of a small Protestant parish at Kaiserswerth on the Rhine. The people were so poor that they could do little either for their church or themselves, so the young pastor set out on foot to seek aid from other Christian people. He traveled in Germany, Holland and England, and everywhere people felt his goodness and gave him help. In London he met Elizabeth Fry, and the noble work she was doing among the prisoners at Newgate made a deep impression on him. He determined to do something to help the prisoners in Germany, especially the poor women, who, after being imprisoned for a certain time, were cast upon the world with no possession save an ill name.

In his little garden stood an old summerhouse, partly ruinous, but with strong walls. With his own hands the good pastor mended the roof and made the place clean and habitable. He put in a bed, a table and a chair, and then prayed that God would send to this shelter some poor soul who needed it.

One night a homeless outcast woman came to the door, and the pastor and his wife bade her welcome, and took her to the clean pleasant room that was all ready.

In this humble way opened the now famous institution of Kaiserswerth. Other poor women soon found out the friendly shelter; in a short time a new and larger building was needed, and more helping hands beside those of the good pastor and his devoted wife. The good work grew and grew; some of the poor women had children, and so a school was started; the school must have good teachers, and so a training school for teachers was opened.

But most of all Pastor Fliedner wished to help the condition of the sick poor; three years after the first opening of the summerhouse shelter in the garden he founded the Deaconess Hospital. We are told that it was opened "practically without patients and without deaconesses." He obtained the use of part of a deserted factory, and begged from his neighbors old furniture and broken crockery, which he mended carefully, and put in the big empty rooms. He had only six sheets, but there was plenty of water to wash them, and when the first patient, a poor suffering servant maid, came to the door, she was made comfortable in a spotless bed, in a clean though bare room.

I wish I could tell you the whole beautiful story, but it would take too long. By the end of the year there were sixty patients in the hospital, and seven deaconess nurses to care for them. To-day there is a deaconess hospital or home in almost every town in Germany, and thousands upon thousands of sick and poor people bless the deaconesses, though they may never have heard the name of Pastor Fliedner.

CHAPTER V

WAITING FOR THE CALL

MISS NIGHTINGALE spent two periods of training at Kaiserswerth. When she left it finally, good Pastor Fliedner laid his hands on her head and gave her his blessing in simple and earnest words; and she carried with her the love and good wishes of all the pious and benevolent community.

I wish we had a picture of her in her deaconess costume. The blue cotton gown, white apron and wide collar, and white muslin cap tied under the chin with a large bow, must have set off her pensive beauty very sweetly. She always kept a tender recollection of Kaiserswerth, and says in a letter: "Never have I met with a higher love and a purer devotion than there."

On her way home, Miss Nightingale spent some time with the Sisters of St. Vincent de Paul in Paris. Here she saw what was probably the best nursing in the world at that time; and she studied the methods in her usual careful way, not only in the hospitals, but in the homes of the poor and suffering, where the good sisters came and went like ministering angels. She had still another opportunity, and this an unsought one, of learning what they had to teach, for she fell ill herself, and was tenderly cared for and restored to health by these skillful and devoted women.

Returning to England, she spent some time in the quiet of home, and as her strength returned, took up her old work of visiting among the sick and poor of the neighborhood. But this could not keep her long. It was not that she did not love it, and did not love her home dearly, but there were other benevolent ladies who could do this work. She realized this, and realized too, though perhaps unconsciously, that she could do harder work than this, and that there was plenty of hard work waiting to be done. She soon found it. A call came asking her to be superintendent of a Home for Sick Governesses in London, and she accepted it at once.

Did you ever think how hard governesses have to work? Did you ever think how tired they must often be, and how their heads must ache—and perhaps their hearts, too—when they are trying to teach you the lessons that you—perhaps again—are not always willing to learn? Well, try to remember, those of you who have your lessons in this way! Remember that you can make the teaching a pain or a pleasure, just as you choose; and that, after all, the teacher is trying to help you, and to give you knowledge that some day you would be very sorry not to have.

In the days of which we are speaking, governesses had a much harder time than nowadays, I think. For one thing, there were not so many different ways in which women could earn their bread. When a girl had to make her own living she went out as a governess almost as a matter of course, whether she had any love for teaching or not, simply because there was nothing else to do. So the teaching was often mere drudgery, and often, too, was not well done; and that meant discontent and unhappiness, and very likely broken health to follow.

The Harley Street Home, as it was then called, was founded to help poor gentlewomen who had lost their health in this kind of life. When Miss Nightingale came to it, things were in a bad condition, owing to lack of means and good management. The friends of the institution were discouraged; but discouragement was a word not to be found in Miss Nightingale's dictionary. There was no money? Well, there must *be* money! She went quietly to work, interested her own friends to subscribe, then talked with the discouraged people, restoring their confidence and inducing them to renew their subscriptions; and soon, with no fuss or flourish of trumpets, the money was in hand.

Then she proceeded, just as quietly, to reorganize the whole institution; engaged competent nurses, arranged the daily life of the inmates, planned and wrote and worked, every day and all day, till she had brought order out of chaos, and made the home, instead of a place of disorder and discontent, one of comfort, peace, and cheerfulness.

You must not think that this was light or pleasant work. Sick and nervous and broken-down women are not easy to deal with; a hospital (for this is what the home really was) is not an easy thing to organize and superintend. It meant, as I have said, hard and vexatious work every day and all day; and I dare say that often and often, when night came, Florence Nightingale lay down to rest more weary than any of her patients.

At length her health gave way under the strain; she broke down, and was forced to give up the work and go home to Embley for a long rest.

It was here, in her own home, amid her own beautiful fields and gardens, that the call came which summoned her to the great work of her life.

CHAPTER VI

THE TRUMPET CALL

Willie, fold your little hands;
    Let it drop—that "soldier" toy;
Look where father's picture stands—
    Father, that here kissed his boy
Not a month since—father kind,
Who this night may—(never mind
Mother's sob, my Willie dear)
Cry out loud that He may hear
Who is God of battles—cry,
"God keep father safe this day
    By the Alma River!"

Ask no more, child. Never heed
    Either Russ, or Frank, or Turk;
Right of nations, trampled creed,
    Chance-poised victory's bloody work;
Any flag i' the wind may roll
On thy heights, Sebastopol!
Willie, all to you and me
Is that spot, whate'er it be,
Where he stands—no other word—
Stands—God sure the child's prayers heard—
    Near the Alma River.

Willie, listen to the bells
    Ringing in the town to-day;
That's for victory. No knell swells
    For the many swept away—
Hundreds, thousands. Let us weep,
We, who need not—just to keep
Reason clear in thought and brain
Till the morning comes again;
Till the third dread morning tell
Who they were that fought and—*fell*
    By the Alma River.

Come, we'll lay us down, my child;
    Poor the bed is—poor and hard;
But thy father, far exiled,
    Sleeps upon the open sward,
Dreaming of us two at home;
Or, beneath the starry dome,
Digs out trenches in the dark,
Where he buries—Willie, mark!
Where *he buries* those who died
Fighting—fighting at his side—
    By the Alma River.

Willie, Willie, go to sleep;
    God will help us, O my boy!
He will make the dull hours creep
    Faster, and send news of joy;
When I need not shrink to meet
Those great placards in the street,
That for weeks will ghastly stare
In some eyes—child, say that prayer
Once again—a different one—
Say "O God! Thy will be done,
    By the Alma River."[1]

---

[1] "By the Alma River," by Dinah Maria Mulock Craik.

PEN your atlas at the map of Russia. Look down toward the bottom, at that part of the great empire which borders on the Euxine or Black Sea; there you will find a small peninsula—it is really almost an island, being surrounded on three sides by water— labeled *"Crimea."* It is only a part of one of the smallest of Russia's forty-odd provinces, the province of Taurida; yet it is one of the famous places of history, for here, in the years 1854 and 1855, was fought the Crimean War, one of the greatest wars of modern times.

Russia and Turkey have never been good neighbors. They have always been jealous of each other, always quarreling about this or that, the fact being that each is afraid of the other's getting too much land and too much power. In these disputes the other countries of Europe have generally sympathized with Turkey, feeling that Russia had quite enough power, and that if she had more it might be dangerous for all of them. Some day you will read in history about the Eastern Question and the Balance of Power, and will find out just what these meant in the Fifties; but this is all that you need know now, in order to understand what I am going to tell you.

In 1854 Turkey, feeling that Russia was pressing too hard upon her, called upon the other European powers to help her. The result was that England, France, Sardinia (now a part of Italy, but then a separate kingdom), and Turkey made an agreement with one another, and all together declared war upon Russia.

England had been at peace with all the world for forty years, ever since the wars of Napoleon, which were closed by the great victory of Waterloo. The English are a brave race; they had forgotten the horrors of war, and remembered only its glories and its victories; and they sprang to arms as joyously as boys run to a football game. "Sharpen your cutlasses, and the day is ours!" said Sir Charles Napier to his men, just before the British fleet sailed; and this was the feeling all through the country.

The fleets of the allied powers gathered in the Black Sea, forming one great armada; surrounded the peninsula of the Crimea, and landed their armies. In September, 1854, was fought the first great battle, by the Alma River. The allies were victorious, and a great shout of joy went up all over England. "Victory! victory!" cried old and young. There were bells and bonfires and illuminations; the whole country went mad with joy, and for a short time no one thought of anything except glory, waving banners and sounding trumpets. But banners and trumpets, though a real part of war, are only a very small part. After a little time, through the shouting and rejoicing a different sound was heard; the sound of weeping and lamentation, not only for the hundreds of brave men who were lying dead beside the fatal river, but for the other hundreds of sick and wounded soldiers, dying for want of care.

There had been gross neglect and terrible mismanagement in the carrying on of the war. Nobody knew just whose fault it was, but everything seemed to be lacking that was most needed on that desolate shore of the Crimea. The English troops were in an enemy's country, and a poor country at that; whatever supplies there were had been taken by the Russian armies for their own needs. Food and clothing had been sent out from England in great quantities, but somehow, no one could find them. Some supplies had been stowed in the hold of vessels, and other things piled on top so that they could not be got at; some were stored in warehouses which no one had authority to open; some were actually rotting at the wharves, for want of precise orders as to their disposal. The surgeons had no bandages, the doctors no medicines; it was a state of things that to-day we can hardly imagine. Indeed, it seemed as if the need were so great and terrible that it paralyzed those who saw it.

"It is now pouring rain," wrote William Howard Russell to the London *Times*, "the skies are black as ink, the wind is howling over the staggering tents, the trenches are turned into dykes; in the tents the water is sometimes a foot deep; our men have not either warm or waterproof clothing; they are out for twelve hours at a time in the trenches; they are plunged into the inevitable miseries of a winter campaign—and not a soul seems to care for their comfort, or even for their lives. These are hard truths, but the people of England must hear them. They must know that the wretched beggar who wanders about the streets of London in the rain, leads the life of a prince compared with the British soldiers who are fighting out here for their country.

*　　　*　　　*　　　*　　　*

"The commonest accessories of a hospital are wanting; there is not the least attention paid to decency or clean linen; the stench is appalling; the fetid air can hardly struggle out to taint the atmosphere, save through the chinks in the walls and roofs; and for all I can observe, these men die without the least effort being made to save them. There they lie, just as they were let gently down on the ground by the poor fellows, their comrades, who brought them on their backs from the camp with the greatest tenderness, but who are not allowed to remain with them. The sick appear to be tended by the sick, and the dying by the dying."

He added that the snow was three feet deep on a level, and the cold so intense that many soldiers were frozen in their tents.

No one meant to be cruel or neglectful; but there were not half enough doctors, and—think of it, children! there were *no nurses.*

How did this happen? Well, when the war broke out the military authorities did not want female nurses. The matter was talked over, and it was decided that things would go better without them. This was put on the ground that the class of nurses, as I have told you, was at that time in England a very poor one. They were often drunken, generally unfeeling, and always ignorant. The War Department decided that this kind of nurse would do more harm than good; they did not realize that "The old order changeth, yielding place to new," and that the time was come when the new nurse must replace the old.

But now the need was come, immediate and terrible, and there was no one to meet it. When the people of England realized this; when they learned that the hospital at Scutari was filled with sick and wounded and dying men, and no one to care for them save a few male orderlies, wholly untrained for the task; when they heard that in the hospitals of the French army the Sisters of Mercy were doing their blessed work, tending the wounded, healing the sick and comforting the dying, and realized that the English soldiers, their own sons, brothers and husbands, had no such help and no such comfort, the sound of bell and trumpet was lost in a great cry of anger and sorrow that went up from the whole country.

And matters grew worse and worse, as one great battle after another sent its dreadful fruits to the already overflowing hospital at Scutari. On October 25th came Balaklava; on November 5th, Inkerman.

You have all read "The Charge of the Light Brigade"; yet I ask you to read it again here, so that it may fit into its place in the story of this terrible war. Remember, it is only one incident of that great battle of Balaklava, in which both sides claimed the victory, while neither gained any signal advantage.

> Half a league, half a league,
>   Half a league onward,
> All in the valley of Death
>   Rode the six hundred.
> "Forward, the Light Brigade!
> Charge for the guns!" he said;

Into the valley of Death
    Rode the six hundred.

"Forward, the Light Brigade!"
Was there a man dismayed?
Not though the solider knew
    Someone had blundered;
Theirs not to make reply,
Theirs not to reason why,
Theirs but to do and die:
Into the valley of Death
    Rode the six hundred.

Cannon to right of them,
Cannon to left of them,
Cannon in front of them
    Volleyed and thundered.
Stormed at with shot and shell,
Boldly they rode and well;
Into the jaws of Death,
Into the mouth of Hell,
    Rode the six hundred.

Flashed all their sabres bare,
Flashed as they turned in air,
Sabring the gunners there,
Charging an army, while
    All the world wondered;
Plunged in the battery-smoke,
Right through the line they broke.
Cossack and Russian

Reeled from the sabre-stroke,
    Shattered and sundered.
Then they rode back, but not—
    Not the six hundred.

Cannon to right of them,
Cannon to left of them,
Cannon behind them
    Volleyed and thundered:
Stormed at with shot and shell,
While horse and hero fell,
They that had fought so well
Came through the jaws of Death
Back from the mouth of Hell—
All that was left of them,
    Left of six hundred.

When can their glory fade?
O the wild charge they made!
    All the world wondered.
Honor the charge they made!
Honor the Light Brigade,
    Noble six hundred![2]

I have already spoken of William Howard Russell. He was the war correspondent of the *Times,* the great English newspaper, and a man of intelligence, heart and feeling. He was on the spot, and saw the horrors of the war at first-hand. His heart was filled with sorrow and pity for the suffering around him, and with indignation that so little was done to relieve it; and he wrote day after day home to England, telling what he saw and what was needed. Soon after Balaklava he wrote:

"Are there no devoted women amongst us, able and willing to go forth to minister to the sick and suffering soldiers of the East in the hospitals at Scutari?

[2] "Charge of the Light Brigade," by Alfred, Lord Tennyson.

Are there none of the daughters of England, at this extreme hour of need, ready for such a work of mercy? France has sent forth her Sisters of Mercy unsparingly, and they are even now by the bedsides of the wounded and the dying, giving what woman's hand alone can give of comfort and relief. Must we fall so far below the French in self-sacrifice and devotedness, in a work which Christ so signally blesses as done unto Himself? 'I was sick and ye visited me.' "

This was the trumpet call that rang in the ears of the women of England, sounding a clearer note than all the clarions of victory. We shall see how it was answered.

CHAPTER VII

THE RESPONSE

MR. SIDNEY HERBERT (afterwards Lord Herbert of Lea) was at this time at the head of the War Department in England. He was a man of noble nature and tender heart, whose whole life was spent in doing good, and in helping those who needed help. He heard with deep distress the dreadful tidings of suffering that came from the Crimea, and his heart responded instantly to the call for help. Yes, the women of England must rise up and go to that far, desolate land to tend and nurse the sick and wounded and dying; but who should lead them? What one woman had the strength, the power, the wisdom, the tenderness, to meet and overcome the terrible conditions? Asking himself this question, Mr. Herbert answered without a moment's hesitation: "Florence Nightingale!"

He knew Miss Nightingale well; she was a dear friend of himself and his beautiful wife, and had again and again given them help and counsel in planning and managing their many charities, hospitals, homes for sick children, and so forth. He knew that she possessed all the qualities needed for this work, and he wrote to her, asking if she would undertake it. Would she, he asked, go out to Scutari, taking with her a band of nurses who would be under her orders, and take charge of the hospital nursing?

He did not make light of the task.

"The selection of the rank and file of nurses would be difficult—no one knows that better than yourself. The difficulty of finding women equal to a task after all full of horror, and requiring, besides intelligence and goodwill, great knowledge and great courage will be great; the task of ruling them and introducing system among them great, and not the least will be the difficulty of making the whole work smoothly with the medical and military authorities out there. This it is which makes it so important that the experiment should be carried out by one with administrative capacity and experience."

He went on to assure Miss Nightingale that she should have full power and authority, and told her frankly that in his opinion she was the one woman in England who was capable of performing this great task.

"I must not conceal from you that upon your decision will depend the ultimate success or failure of the plan. . . . If this succeeds, an enormous amount of good will be done now, and to persons deserving everything at our hands; and which will multiply the good to all time."

It was a noble letter, this of Mr. Herbert's, but he might have spared himself the trouble of writing it. Florence Nightingale, in her quiet country home, had heard the call to the women of England; and even while Mr. Herbert was composing his letter to her, she was writing to him, a brief note, simply offering her services in the hospitals at Scutari. Her letter crossed his on the way; and the next day it was proclaimed from the War Office that Miss Nightingale, "a lady with greater practical experience of hospital administration and treatment than any other lady in the country," had been appointed by Government to the office of Superintendent of Nurses at Scutari, and had undertaken the work of organizing and taking out nurses thither.

Great was the amazement in England. Nothing of this kind had ever been heard of before. "Who is Miss Nightingale?" people cried all over the country. They were answered by the newspapers. First the *Examiner* and then the *Times* told them that Miss Nightingale was " a young lady of singular endowments both natural and acquired. In a knowledge of the ancient languages and of the higher branches of mathematics, in general art, science, and literature, her attainments are extraordinary. There is scarcely a modern language which she does not understand, and she speaks French, German and Italian as fluently as her native English. She has visited and studied all the various nations of Europe, and has ascended the Nile to its remotest cataract. Young (about the age of our Queen), graceful, feminine, rich, popular, she holds a singularly gentle and persuasive influence over all with whom she comes in contact. Her friends and acquaintances are of all classes and persuasions, but her happiest place is at home, in the centre of a very large band of accomplished relatives, and in simplest obedience to her admiring parents."

One who knew our heroine well wrote in a more personal vein:

"Miss Nightingale is one of those whom God forms for great ends. You cannot hear her say a few sentences—no, not even look at her, without feeling that she is an extraordinary being. Simple, intellectual, sweet, full of love and benevolence, she is a fascinating and perfect woman. She is tall and pale. Her face is exceedingly lovely; but better than all is the soul's glory that shines through every feature so exultingly. Nothing can be sweeter than her smile. It is like a sunny day in summer."

Though well known among a large circle of earnest and high-minded persons, Miss Nightingale's name was entirely new to the English people as a whole, and—everything else apart—they were delighted with its beauty. Had she been plain Mary Smith, she would have done just as good work, but it would have been far harder for her to start it. Florence Nightingale was a name to conjure with, as the saying is, and it echoed far and wide. Everybody who could write verses (and many who could not), began instantly to write about nightingales. *Punch* printed a cartoon showing a hospital ward, with the "ladybirds" hovering about the cots of the sick men, each bird having a nurse's head. Another picture represented one of the bird-nurses flying through the air, carrying in her claws a jug labeled "Fomentation, Embrocation, Gruel." This was called "The Jug of the Nightingale," for many people think that some of the bird's beautiful, liquid notes sound like "jug, jug, jug!"

Not content with pictures, *Punch* printed "The Nightingale's Song to the Sick Soldier," which became very popular, and was constantly quoted in those days.

Listen, soldier, to the tale of the tender nightingale,
　　'Tis a charm that soon will ease your wounds so cruel,
Singing medicine for your pain, in a sympathetic strain,
　　With a jug, jug, jug of lemonade or gruel.

Singing bandages and lint; salve and cerate without stint,
　　Singing plenty both of liniment and lotion,
And your mixtures pushed about, and the pills for you served
　　　　out
　　With alacrity and promptitude of motion.

Singing light and gentle hands, and a nurse who understands
　　How to manage every sort of application,
From a poultice to a leech; whom you haven't got to teach
　　The way to make a poppy fomentation.

Singing pillow for you, smoothed; smart and ache and
　　　　anguish soothed,
　　By the readiness of feminine invention;
Singing fever's thirst allayed, and the bed you've tumbled
　　　　made
　　With a cheerful and considerate attention.

Singing succour to the brave, and a rescue from the grave,
　　Hear the nightingale that's come to the Crimea;
'Tis a nightingale as strong in her heart as in her song,
　　To carry out so gallant an idea.

Of course there were some people who shook their heads; there always are when any new work is undertaken. Some thought it was improper for women to nurse in a military hospital; others thought they would be useless, or worse; others again thought that the nurses would ruin their own health and be sent home in a month to the hospitals of England. There were still other objections, which were strongly felt in those days, however strange they may sound in our ears to-day.

"Oh, dreadful!" said some people; "Miss Nightingale is a Unitarian!"

"Oh, shocking!" said others. "Miss Nightingale is a Roman Catholic!" And so it went on. But while they were talking and exclaiming, drawing pictures and singing songs, Miss Nightingale was getting ready. In six days from the time she undertook the work she was ready to start, with thirty nurses, chosen with infinite care and pains from the hundreds who had volunteered to go. There was no flourish of trumpets. While England was still wondering how they could go, and whether they ought to be allowed to go—behold, they were gone! slipping away by night, as if they were bound on some secret errand. Indeed, Miss Nightingale has never been able to endure "fuss and feathers," and all her life she has looked for a bushel large enough to hide her light under, though happily she has never succeeded.

Only a few relatives and near friends stood on the railway platform on that evening of October 21, 1854. Miss Nightingale, simply dressed in black, was very quiet, very serene, with a cheerful word for everyone; no one who saw her parting look and smile ever forgot them. So, in night and silence, the "Angel Band" whose glory was soon to shine over all the world, left the shores of England.

But though England slept that night, France was wide awake the next morning. The fishwives of Boulogne had heard what was doing across the Channel, and were on the lookout. When Miss Nightingale and her nurses stepped ashore they were met by a band of women, in snowy caps and rainbow-striped petticoats, all with outstretched hands, all crying, "Welcome, welcome, our English sisters!"

They knew, Marie and Jeanne and Suzette. Their own husbands, sons, and brothers were fighting and dying in the Crimea; their own nurses, the blessed Sisters of Mercy, had from the first been toiling in hospital and trench in that dreadful land; how should they not welcome the English sisters who were going to join in the holy work?

Loudly they proclaimed that none but themselves, the fishwives of Boulogne, should help the *soeurs Anglaises*. They shouldered bag and baggage; they swung the heavy trunks up on their broad backs, and with laughter and tears mingled in true French fashion, trudged away to the railway station. Pay? Not a sou; not a centime! The blessing of our English sisters is all we desire; and if they should chance to see Pierre or Jacques *là-bas*—ah! the heavens are over all. A handshake, then, and *Adieu! Adieu! vivent les soeurs!* the good God go with you!

And that prayer was surely answered.

CHAPTER VIII

SCUTARI

OPEN the atlas once more at the map of Russia, and look downward from the Crimea, across the Black Sea toward the southwest. You see a narrow strait marked "Bosporus" leading from the Black Sea to the Sea of Marmora; and on either side of the strait a black dot, one marked "Constantinople," the other "Scutari." It is to Scutari that we are going, but we must not pass the other places without a word, for they are very famous. This is the land of story, and every foot of ground, every trickle of water, has its legend or fairy tale, or true story of sorrow or heroism.

Bosporus means "the cow's ford." It was named, the old story says, for Io, a beautiful maiden beloved of Zeus. To conceal her from the eyes of Hera, his jealous wife, Zeus turned Io into a snow-white heifer; but Hera, suspecting the truth, persuaded him to give the poor pretty creature to her. Then followed a sad time. Hera set Argus, a giant with a hundred eyes, to watch the heifer, lest she escape and regain her human form. The poor heifer-maiden was so unhappy that Zeus sent Hermes to set her free; and

53

the cunning god told stories to Argus till he fell asleep, and then cut off his head, hundred eyes and all. Hera took the eyes and put them in the tail of her sacred peacock, and there they are to this day. Meantime Io ran away as fast as she could, but she could not escape the vengeance of the jealous goddess. Hera sent a gad-fly after her, which stung her cruelly, and pursued her over land and sea. The poor creature fled wildly hither and thither; swam across the Ionian Sea, which has borne her name ever since; roamed over the whole breadth of what is now Turkey, and finally came to the narrow strait or ford between the two seas. Here she crossed again, and went on her weary way; and here again she left—not her own name, but that of the animal in whose form she suffered. Poor Io! one is glad to read that she was released at last, and given her woman's body again. True? No, the story is not true, but it is very famous. Those of you who care about moths will find another reminder of Io in the beautiful *Saturnia* Io, which is named for the Greek maiden and her cruel foe, Saturnia being another name for Hera or Juno.

The scenery along the banks of the Bosporus is so beautiful that whole books have been written about it. On either side are seven promontories and seven bays; indeed, it is almost a chain of seven lakes, connected by seven swift-rushing currents. The promontories are crowned with villages, towns, palaces, ruins, each with its own beauty, its own interest, its own story; but we cannot stay for these; we must go onward to where, at the lower end of the passage, with its

54

long, narrow harbor, the Golden Horn, curling round it, lies Constantinople, the wonder-city.

Here indeed we must stop for a moment, for this is one of the most famous cities of history. In ancient days, when Rome was in her glory and long before, it was Byzantium that lay shining in the curve of the Golden Horn; Byzantium the rich, the powerful, the desired of all; fought over through successive generations by Persian, Greek, Gaul and Roman; conquered, liberated, conquered again. In the second century of our era it was besieged by the Roman emperor Severus, and after a heroic resistance lasting three years, was taken and laid waste by the conqueror. But the city sprang up again, more beautiful than ever, and a century and a half later the emperor Constantine made it the capital of the Roman Empire, and gave it his own name.

Constantinopolis, the City of Constantine ; so it became in the year 330, and so it remains to this day, but not under the rule of Romans or their descendants.

"Blessed shall he be who shall take Constantinople!" So, three hundred years later, exclaimed Mohammed, the prophet and leader of men. His disciples and followers never forgot the saying, and many wars were fought, many desperate attempts made by the Mohammedans to win the wonder city. It was another Mohammed, not a prophet but a great soldier, surnamed the Conqueror, who finally conquered it, in 1453, after another tremendous siege, of which you will read in history. There is a terrible story about the entry of this savage conqueror into the city. It is said that its inhabitants, mostly Christians, though of various nationalities, took refuge in the great church of St. Sophia, and were there barbarously slaughtered by the ferocious Turks. In the south aisle of the church the dead lay piled in great heaps, and in over this dreadful rampart rode Mohammed on his war horse; and as he rode, he lifted his bloody right hand and smote one of the pillars, and there—so the story says—the mark may be seen to this day.

From that time to our own Constantinople has been the capital city of the Turkish Empire. Again, I wish I might tell you about at least a few of its many wonders, for I have seen some of them, but again I must hasten on.

The city is so great that it overflows in every direction; in fact, there are three cities in one: Stamboul, the central division, filling the tongue of land between the Golden Horn and the Sea of Marmora; Galata, on the farther bank of the Horn; and Scutari, on the opposite shore of the Bosporus. It is to the last-named that we are going.

Although actually a suburb of Constantinople, Scutari is a town in itself, and a large and ancient one. In the earliest times of the great Persian monarchy, it was called *Chrysopolis,* the Golden City. Its present name means in Persian a courier who carries royal orders from station to station; that is because the place has always, from its earliest days, been a *rendezvous* for caravans, messengers, travelers of every description. Here Xenophon and his Greeks, returning from the war against Cyrus, halted for seven days while the sol-

diers disposed of the booty they had won in the campaign. Here, for hundreds of years, stood the three co-
lossal statues, forty-eight feet high, erected by the
Byzantians in honor of the Athenians, who had saved
them from destruction at the hands of Philip the Lace-
daemonian. Here, to-day, are mosques and convents,
palaces and tombs, especially the last; for the burying
ground of Scutari is one of the largest in the world,
and its silent avenues hold, some say, twenty times as
many dwellers as the gay and noisy streets of Stamboul.

It is a strange place, this great burying ground.
Beside each tomb rises a cypress tree, tall and majestic.
The tombs themselves are mostly pillars of marble,
with a globe or ball on the top; and perched atop of
this globe is in many cases a turban or a fez, carved in
stone and painted in gay colors. This shows that a man
lies beneath; the women's tombs are marked by a
grapevine or a stem of lotus, also carved in marble. At
foot of the column is a flat stone, hollowed out in the
middle to form a small basin. Some of these basins are
filled with flowers or perfumes; in others, the rain and
dew make a pleasant bathing and drinking place for the
birds who fly in great flocks about the quiet place.

Not far from this great cemetery is another
place of burial, that of the English ; and this is laid out
like a lovely garden, and watched and tended with loving care; for here rest the brave men who fell in this
terrible war of the Crimea, or who wasted away in the
great building that towers foursquare over all the
neighborhood. We must look well at this building, the
Barrack Hospital of Scutari, for this is what Florence

Nightingale came so far to see. Through all the long, wearisome journey, I doubt whether she gave much heed to the beauties or the discomforts of the way. Her eyes were set steadfastly forward, following her swift thoughts; and eyes and thoughts sought this one thing, this gaunt, bare building rising beside the new-made graves. Let us follow her and see what she found there.

CHAPTER IX

THE BARRACK HOSPITAL

HE Barrack Hospital at Scutari was just what its name implies. It was built for soldiers to live in, and was big enough to take in whole regiments. Surrounding the four sides of a quadrangle, each one of its sides was nearly a quarter of a mile long, and it was believed that twelve thousand men could be exercised in the great central court. Three sides of the building were arranged in galleries and corridors, rising story upon story; we are told that these long narrow rooms, if placed end to end, would cover four miles of ground. At each corner rose a tower; the building was well situated, and looked out over the Bosporus toward the glittering mosques and minarets of Stamboul.

You would think that this vast building would hold all the sick and wounded men of one short war; but this was not so. Seven others were erected, and all were filled to overflowing ; but the Barrack Hospital was Miss Nightingale's headquarters, and the chief scene of her labors, though she had authority over all; I shall therefore describe the situation and the work as she found it there.

If there had been mismanagement at home in England, there had been even worse at the seat of war. The battles, you remember, were all fought in the Crimea. They were cruel, terrible battles, too terrible to dwell upon here. Hundreds and thousands were killed; but other hundreds and thousands lay wounded and helpless on the field. In those days there was no Red Cross, no field practice, no first aid to the injured. The poor sufferers were taken, all bleeding and fainting as they were, to the water side, and there put in boats which carried them, tossing on the rough waters of the Black Sea, across to Scutari. Several days would pass before any were got from the battlefield to the ferry below the hospital, and most of them had not had their wounds dressed or their broken limbs set. Often they had had no food; they were tortured by fever and thirst; and now they must walk, if they could drag themselves, or be dragged or carried by others up the hill to the hospital. We can fancy how they looked forward to rest; how they thought of comfort, aid, relief from pain. Alas! they found little of all these things.

The Barrack Hospital had been built by the Turks, and lent to the English by the Turkish Government; it had been meant for the hardy Turkish soldiery to sleep in, and there were no appliances to fit it for a hospital. We are told that in the early months of the war "there were no vessels for water or utensils of any kind; no soap, towels or cloths, no hospital clothes; the men lying in their uniforms, stiff with gore and covered with filth to a degree and of a kind no one could write about; their persons covered with vermin, which crawled about the floors and walls of the dreadful den of dirt, pestilence and death to which they were consigned."

Is this too dreadful to read about? But it was not too dreadful to happen. The poor fellows, laid down in the midst of all this horror, would wait with a soldier's patience, hoping for the doctor or surgeon who should bind up their wounds and relieve their terrible suffering. Alas! often and often death was more prompt than the doctor, and stilled the pain forever, before any human aid had been given.

One of Miss Nightingale's assistants writes:

"How can I ever describe my first day in the hospital at Scutari? Vessels were arriving and orderlies carrying the poor fellows, who with their wounds and frost-bites had been tossing about on the Black Sea for two or three days and sometimes more. Where were they to go? Not an available bed. They were laid on the floor one after another, till the beds were emptied of those dying of cholera and every other disease. Many died immediately after being brought in—their moans would pierce the heart—and the look of agony on those poor dying faces will never leave my heart. They may well be called 'the martyrs of the Crimea.' "

Where were the doctors? They were there, doing their very best; working day and night, giving their strength and their lives freely; but there were not half, not a tenth part, enough of them; and there was no one to help them but the orderlies, who, as I have said, had had no training, and knew nothing of sickness or hospital work. The conditions grew so frightful that a kind of paralysis seemed to fall upon the minds of the workers. They felt that the task was hopeless, and they went about their duties like people in a nightmare. The strangest thing of all, to us now, seems to be that they *did not tell.* Though Mr. Russell and others wrote to England of the horrors of the hospitals, the authorities themselves were silent, or if questioned, would only reply that everything was "all right." There was no inspection that was worthy of the name. The same officers who would front death on the battlefield with a song and a laugh, shrank from meeting it in the hospital wards, the air of which was heavy with the poison of cholera and fever.

"An orderly officer took the rounds of the wards every night, to see that all was in order. He was of course expected by the orderlies, and the moment he raised the latch he received the word: 'All right, your honor!' and passed on. This was hospital inspection!"[3]

In fact, these orderlies too often, I fear, bore some resemblance to the old class of nurses that I described, and were in many cases rough, unfeeling, ignorant men. Sometimes it was for this reason that they drank the brandy which should have been given to their patients; but often, again, it was because they were ill themselves, or else because they were so overcome by the horrors around them that they drank just to bring forgetfulness for a time.

The strange paralysis of which I have spoken seemed to hang over everything connected with the unfortunate soldiers of the Crimea. Mr. Sidney Herbert

[3] Tooley, "Life of Florence Nightingale," p. 137.

assured Miss Nightingale that the hospitals were supplied with every necessary. He had reason to think so,
for the things had been sent, had left England, had
reached the shores of the Bosporus. "Medical stores
had been sent out by the ton." But where were they? I
have already told you; they were rotting on the
wharves, locked up in the warehouses, buried in the
holds of vessels; they were everywhere except in the
hospitals. The doctors had nothing to work with, but
they could not leave their work to find out why it was.

The other authorities said it was "all right!"
They knew the things had come, but they were not
sure just who were the proper persons to open the
cargoes, take out and distribute the stores; it must not
be done except by the proper persons. This is what is
called *red tape;* it stands for authority without intelligence, and many books have been written about it. I
remember, when I was a child, a cartoon in *Punch*
showing the British soldier entangled in the coils of a
frightful serpent, struggling for life; the serpent was
labeled *"Red Tape."* (The monster is still alive in our
day, but he is not nearly so powerful, and people are
always on the lookout for him, and can generally drive
him away.)

This was the state of things when Miss Nightingale and her band of nurses arrived at Scutari. Her first
round of the hospitals was a terrible experience, which
no later one ever effaced from her mind. The air of the
wards was so polluted as to be perfectly stifling. "The
sheets," she said, "were of canvas, and so coarse that
the wounded men begged to be left in their blankets. It
was indeed impossible to put men in such a state of

emaciation into those sheets. There was no bedroom furniture of any kind, and only empty beer or wine bottles for candlesticks."[4]

The wards were full to overflowing, and the corridors crowded with sick and wounded, lying on the floor, with the rats running over them. She looked out of the windows; under them were lying dead animals in every state of decay, refuse and filth of every description. She sought the kitchens; there were no kitchens, and no cooks; at least nothing that would be recognized to-day as a hospital kitchen. In the barrack kitchen were thirteen huge coppers; in these the men cooked their own food, meat and vegetables together, the separate portions inclosed in nets, all plunged in together, and taken out when some one was ready to take them. Part of the food would be raw when it came out, another part boiled to rags. This was all the food there was, for sick and well, the wounded, the fever-stricken, the cholera patient. No doubt hundreds died from improper feeding alone.

She looked for the laundry; there was no laundry. There were washing contracts, but up to the time of her arrival "only seven shirts had been washed." The clothes and bed linen of wounded men and of those sick with infectious diseases were thrown in together. Moreover, the contractors stole most of the clothes that came into their hands, so that the sick did not like to part with their few poor garments, for fear of never seeing them again, and were practically without clean linen, except when a soldier's wife would

---

[4] Tooley, "Life of Florence Nightingale," p. 126.

now and then take compassion on them, and wash out a few articles.

These were the conditions that Florence Nightingale had to meet. A delicate and sensitive woman, reared amid beauty and luxury, these were the scenes among which she was to live for nearly two years. But one thing more must be noted. Do you think everyone was glad to see her and her nurses? Not by any means! The overwrought doctors were dismayed and angered at the prospect of a "parcel of women" coming—as they fancied—to interfere with their work, and make it harder than it was already. The red-tape officials were even less pleased. What? A woman in petticoats, a "Lady-in-Chief," coming to inquire into their deeds and their methods? Had they not said repeatedly that everything was all right? What was the meaning of this?

This was her coming; this is what she found; now we shall see what she did.

CHAPTER X

THE LADY-IN-CHIEF

ISS NIGHTINGALE arrived at Scutari on November 4th. You have seen what she found; but there was worse to come. Only twenty-four hours after her arrival, the wounded from the battle of Inkerman began to come in; soon every inch of room in both the Barrack and the General hospital was full, and men by hundreds were lying on the muddy ground outside, unable to find room even on the floor of the corridor. Neither Lady-in-Chief nor nurses had had time to rest after their long voyage, to make plans for systematic work, even to draw breath after their first glimpse of the horrors around them, when this great avalanche of suffering and misery came down upon them. No woman in history has had to face such a task as now flung itself upon Florence Nightingale.

She met it as the great meet trial, quietly and calmly. Her cheek might pale at what she had to see, but there was no flinching in those clear, gray-blue eyes, no trembling of those firm lips. Ship after ship discharged its ghastly freight at the ferry below; train after train of wounded was dragged up the hill, brought into the overflowing hospital, laid down on pallet, on mattress, on bare floor, on muddy ground, wherever space could be found. "The men lay in double rows down the long corridors, forming several miles of suffering humanity."

As the poor fellows were brought in, they looked up, and saw a slender woman in a black dress, with a pale, beautiful face surmounted by a close-fitting white cap. Quietly, but with an authority that no one ever thought of disputing, she gave her orders, directing where the sufferers were to be taken, what doctor was to be summoned, what nurses to attend them. During these days she was known sometimes to stand on her feet *twenty hours at a time*, seeing that each man was put in the right place, where he might receive the right kind of help. I ask you to think of this for a moment. Twenty hours nearly the whole of a day and night.

Where a particularly severe operation was to be performed, Miss Nightingale was present whenever it was possible, giving to both surgeon and patient the comfort and support of her wonderful calm strength and sympathy. In this dreadful inrush of the Inkerman wounded, the surgeons had first of all to separate the more hopeful cases from those that seemed desperate. The working force was so insufficient, they must devote their energies to saving those who could be saved; this is how it seemed to them. Once Miss Nightingale saw five men lying together in a corner, left just as they had come from the vessel.

"Can nothing be done for them?" she asked the surgeon in charge. He shook his head.

"Then will you give them to me?"

"Take them," replied the surgeon, "if you like; but we think their case is hopeless."

Do you remember the little girl sitting by the wounded dog? All night long Florence Nightingale sat beside those five men, one of the faithful nurses with her, feeding them with a spoon at short intervals till consciousness returned, and a little strength began to creep back into their poor torn bodies; then washing their wounds, making them tidy and decent, and all the time cheering them with kind and hopeful words. When morning came the surgeons, amazed, pronounced the men in good condition to be operated upon, and—we will hope, though the story does not tell the end—saved.

Is it any wonder that one poor lad burst into tears as he cried: "I can't help it, I can't indeed, when I see them. Only think of Englishwomen coming out here to nurse us! It seems so homelike and comfortable."

In those days one of the nurses wrote home to England:

"It does appear absolutely impossible to meet the wants of those who are dying of dysentery and exhaustion; out of four wards committed to my care, eleven men have died in the night, simply from exhaustion, which, humanly speaking, might have been stopped, could I have laid my hand at once on such nourishment as I knew they ought to have had.

"It is necessary to be as near the scene of war as we are, to know the horrors which we have seen and heard of. I know not which sight is most heart-rending—to witness fine strong men and youths worn down by exhaustion and sinking under it, or others coming in fearfully wounded.

"The whole of yesterday was spent, first in sewing the men's mattresses together, and then in washing them, and assisting the surgeons, when we could, in dressing their ghastly wounds, and seeing the poor fellows made as easy as their circumstances would admit of, after their five days' confinement on board ship, during which space their wounds were not dressed. . . . We have not seen a drop of milk, and the bread is extremely sour. The butter is most filthy—it is Irish butter in a state of decomposition; and the meat is more like moist leather than food. Potatoes we are waiting for until they arrive from France."

This was written six days after arrival. By the tenth day, a miracle had been accomplished. Miss Nightingale had established and fitted up a kitchen, from which eight hundred men were fed daily with delicacies and food suitable to their condition. Beef-tea, chicken broth, jelly—a quiet wave of the wand, and these things sprang up, as it were, out of the earth.

Hear how one of the men describes it himself. On arriving at the hospital early in the morning, he was given a bowl of gruel. " 'Tommy, me boy,' he said to himself, 'that's all you'll get into your inside this blessed day, and think yourself lucky you've got that.' But two hours later, if another of them blessed angels didn't come entreating of me to have just a little chicken broth! Well, I took that, thinking maybe it was early dinner, and before I had well done wondering what would happen next, round the nurse came again with a bit o' jelly, and all day long at intervals they kept on bringing me what they called 'a little nourishment.' In the evening, Miss Nightingale she came and had a look at me, and says she, 'I hope you're feeling better.' I could have said, 'Ma'am, I feels as fit as a fightin' cock,' but I managed to git out somethin' a bit more polite."

How was the miracle accomplished? Up to this time, the method of giving out stores had been much like the method (only there was really no method about it!) of cooking and washing. There were no regular hours; if you asked for a thing in the morning, you might get it in the evening, when the barrack fires were out. And you could get nothing at all until it had been inspected by this official, approved by that, and finally given out by the other. These were called "service rules"; they were really folds and coils of the monster Red Tape, at his work of binding and strangling. How was the miracle accomplished? Simply enough. Miss Nightingale, with the foresight of a born leader, had anticipated all this, and was ready for it. The materials for all the arrowroot, beef-tea, chicken broth, wine jelly, of those first weeks, came out of her own stores, brought out with her in the vessel, the *Victis,* from England. She had no intention of waiting a day or an hour for anyone; she had not a day or an hour to waste.

It must have been a wonderful cargo, that of the *Victis;* I can think of nothing but the astonishing bag of the Mother in the "Swiss Family Robinson," or that still more marvelous one of the Fairy Blackstick. Do you remember?

"And Giglio returned to his room, where the first thing he saw was the fairy bag lying on the table, which seemed to give a little hop as he came in. 'I hope it has some breakfast in it,' says Giglio, 'for I have only a very little money left.' But on opening the bag, what do you think was there? A blacking-brush and a pot of Warren's jet, and on the pot was written,

> "Poor young men their boots must black;
> Use me and cork me and put me back!"

So Giglio laughed and blacked his boots, and put the brush and the bottle into the bag.

"When he had done dressing himself, the bag gave another hop, and he went to it and took out—

1. A tablecloth and napkin.
2. A sugar basin full of the best loaf sugar.
4, 6, 8, 10. Two forks, two teaspoons, two knives, and a pair of sugar-tongs, and a butterknife, all marked G.
11, 12, 13. A teacup, saucer, and slop-basin.
14. A jug full of delicious cream.
15. A canister with black tea and green.
16. A large tea-urn and boiling water.

17. A saucepan, containing three eggs nicely done.
18. A quarter of a pound of best Epping butter.
19. A brown loaf.

"And if he hadn't enough now for a good breakfast, I should like to know who ever had one?"

When I was your age, I never tired of reading about this breakfast; and then there was that other wonderful day when the bag was "grown so long that the Prince could not help remarking it. He went to it, opened it, and what do you think he found in it?

"A splendid long gold-handled, red-velvet-scabbarded cut-and-thrust sword, and on the sheath was embroidered 'ROSALBA FOREVER!' "

But I am not writing the "Rose and the Ring"; I wish I were!

So, as I said, all good and comforting things came in those first days out of the Fairy Florence's bag—I mean ship. She hired a house close by the hospital, and set up a laundry, with every proper and sanitary arrangement, and there, every week, five hundred shirts were washed, besides other garments. But now came a new difficulty. Many of the soldiers had no clothes at all save the filthy and ragged ones on their backs; what was to become of them while their shirts were washed and mended? The ship bag gave another hop (at least I should think it would have, for pure joy of the good it was doing), and out came ten thousand shirts; and for the first time since they left the battlefield the sick and wounded men were clean and comfortable.

But the Lady-in-Chief knew that her fairy stores were not of the kind that renew themselves; and having once got matters into something like decent order and comfort in the hospital, she turned quietly and resolutely to do battle with the monster Red Tape.

The officials of Scutari did not know what to make of the new state of things. As I have said, many of them had shaken their heads and pulled very long faces when they heard that a woman was coming out who was to have full power and authority over all things pertaining to the care of the sick and wounded. They honestly thought, no doubt, that the confusion would be doubled, the distraction turned to downright madness. What could a woman know about such matters? What experience had she had of "service rules"? What would become of them all?

They were soon to find out. The Lady-in-Chief did not cry out, or wring her hands, or do any of the things they had expected. Neither did she bluster or rage, scold or reproach. She simply said that this or that must be done, and then saw that it was done. Her tact and judgment were as great as her power and wisdom; more I cannot say.

Suppose she wanted certain stores that were in a warehouse on the wharf. The warehouse was locked. She sent for the wharfinger. Would he please open the warehouse and give her the stores? He was very sorry, but he could not do so without an order from the board. She went to the chief officer of the board. He was very sorry, but it would be necessary to have a meeting of the entire board. Who made up the board? Well, Mr. So-and-so, and Dr. This, and Mr. That, and Colonel 'Tother. Where were they? Well, one of them was not very well, and another was probably out riding, and a third—

Would he please call them together at once?

Well, he was extremely busy just now, but tomorrow or the day after, he would be delighted—

Would he be ready himself for a meeting, if Miss Nightingale could get the other members of the board together? Well—of course—he would be delighted, but he could assure Miss Nightingale that everything would be all right, without her having the trouble to—

The board met; pen, ink and paper were ready. Would they kindly sign the order? Many thanks! Good morning!

And the warehouse was opened, and the goods on their way to the hospital, before the astonished gentlemen had fairly drawn their breath.

"But what kind of way is this to do business?" cried the slaves of Red Tape. "She doesn't give us time! The moment a thing is wanted, she goes and gets it!!! The rules of the service—"

But this was not true; for, as methodical as she was wise and generous, Miss Nightingale was most careful to consult the proper authorities, and, whenever it was possible, to make them take the necessary steps themselves. Once, and only once, did she absolutely take the law into her own hands. There came a moment when certain stores were desperately needed for some sick and wounded men. The stores were at hand, but they had not been inspected, and Red Tape had decreed that nothing should be given out until it had been inspected by the board. (This was another board, probably; their name was Legion.) Miss Nightingale tried to get the board together, but this time without success. One was away, and another was ill, and a third was—I don't know where. The clear gray-blue eyes grew stern.

"I must have these things!" she said quietly. "My men are dying for lack of them."

The under-official stammered and turned pale; he did not wish to disobey her, but—it meant a court-martial for him if he disobeyed the rules of the service.

"You shall have no blame," said the Lady-in-Chief. "I take the entire responsibility upon myself. Open the door!"

The door was opened, and in a few moments the sick men had the stimulants for lack of which they were sinking into exhaustion.

When Miss Nightingale arrived at Scutari, the death rate in the Barrack Hospital was sixty per cent; within a few months it was reduced to one per cent; and this, under heaven, was accomplished by her and her devoted band of nurses. Do you wonder that she was called "The Angel of the Crimea?"

CHAPTER XI

THE LADY WITH THE LAMP

Whene'er a noble deed is wrought;
Whene'er is spoken a noble thought,
    Our hearts, in glad surprise,
    To higher levels rise.

The tidal wave of deeper souls
Into our inmost being rolls,
    And lifts us unawares
    Out of all meaner cares.

Honor to those whose words or deeds
Thus help us in our daily needs,
    And by their overflow
    Raise us from what is low!

Thus thought I, as by night I read
Of the great army of the dead,
    The trenches cold and damp,
    The starved and frozen camp,—

The wounded from the battle-plain,
In dreary hospitals of pain,
    The cheerless corridors,
    The cold and stony floors.

THE LADY WITH THE LAMP

Lo! in that house of misery
A lady with a lamp I see
    Pass through the glimmering gloom,
    And flit from room to room.

And slow, as in a dream of bliss,
The speechless sufferer turns to kiss
    Her shadow, as it falls
    Upon the darkening walls.

As if a door in heaven should be
Opened and then closed suddenly,
    The vision came and went,
    The light shone and was spent.

On England's annals, through the long
Hereafter of her speech and song,
    That light its rays shall cast
    From portals of the past.

A Lady with a Lamp shall stand
In the great history of the land,
    A noble type of good,
    Heroic womanhood.

Nor even shall be wanting here
The palm, the lily, and the spear,
    The symbols that of yore
    Saint Filomena bore.[5]

[5] "Santa Filomena," by Henry Wadsworth Longfellow.

ISS NIGHTINGALE'S headquarters were in the "Sisters' Tower," as it came to be called, one of the four corner towers of the great building. Here was a large, airy room, with doors opening off it on each side. In the middle was a large table, covered with stores of every kind, constantly in demand, constantly replaced; and on the floor, and flowing into all the corners, were—more stores! Bales of shirts, piles of socks, slippers, dressing gowns, sheets, flannels—everything you can think of that is useful and comfortable in time of sickness. About these piles the white-capped nurses came and went, like bees about a hive; all was quietly busy, cheerful, methodical. In a small room opening off the large one the Lady-in-Chief held her councils with nurses, doctors, generals or orderlies; giving to all the same courteous attention, the same clear, calm, helpful advice or directions. Here, too, for hours at a time, she sat at her desk, writing; letters to Sidney Herbert and his wife; letters to Lord Raglan, the commander-in-chief, who, though at first averse to her coming, became one of her firmest friends and admirers; letters to sorrowing wives and mothers and sisters in England. She received letters by the thousand; she could not answer them all with her own hand, but I am sure she answered as many as was possible. One letter was forwarded to her by the Herberts which gave a great pleasure not to her only, but to everyone in all that place of suffering. It was dated Windsor Castle, December 6, 1854.

"Would you tell Mrs. Herbert," wrote good Queen Victoria, "that I beg she would let me see frequently the accounts she receives from Miss Nightingale or Mrs. Bracebridge, as *I hear no details of the wounded,* though I see so many from officers, etc., about the battlefield, and naturally the former must interest *me* more than anyone.

"Let Mrs. Herbert also know that I wish Miss Nightingale and the ladies would tell these poor, noble wounded and sick men, that *no one* takes a warmer interest or feels *more* for their sufferings or admires their courage and heroism *more* than their Queen. Day and night she thinks of her beloved troops. So does the Prince.

"Beg Mrs. Herbert to communicate these my words to those ladies, as I know that *our* sympathy is much valued by these noble fellows.—Victoria."

I think the tears may have come into those clear eyes of Miss Nightingale, when she read these words. She gave the letter to one of the chaplains, and he went from ward to ward, reading it aloud to the men, and ending each reading with "God save the Queen!" The words were murmured or whispered after him by the lips of sick and dying, and through all the mournful place went a great wave of tender love and loyalty toward the good Queen in England, and toward their own queen, their angel, who had shared her pleasure with them.

You will hardly believe that in England, while the Queen was writing thus, some people were still sadly troubled about Miss Nightingale's religious views, and were writing to the papers, warning other people against her; but so it was. One clergyman actually warned his flock not to subscribe money for the soldiers in the East "if it was to pass through Popish hands." He thought the Lady-in-Chief was a Catholic; others still maintained that she was a Unitarian; others were sure she had gone out with the real purpose of converting the soldiers to High-Church views.

In reading about this kind of thing, it is comforting to find one good Irish clergyman who, being asked to what sect Miss Nightingale belonged, replied: "She belongs to a sect which unfortunately is a very rare one—the sect of the Good Samaritans."

But these grumblers were only a few, we must think. The great body of English people was filled with an enthusiasm of gratitude toward the "angel band" and its leader. From the Queen in her palace down to the humblest working women in her cottage, all were at work making lint and bandages, shirts and socks and havelocks for the soldiers. Nor were they content with making things. Every housekeeper ransacked her linen closet and camphor chest, piled sheets and blankets and pillowcases together, tied them up in bundles, addressed them to Miss Nightingale, and sent them off.

When Sister Mary Aloysius first began to sort the bales of goods on the wharf at Scutari, she thought that "the English nobility must have emptied their wardrobes and linen stores, to send out bandages for the wounded. There was the most beautiful underclothing, and the finest cambric sheets, with merely a scissors run here and there through them, to insure their being used for no other purpose, some from the Queen's palace, with the royal monogram beautifully worked."

Yes, and the rats had a wonderful time with all these fine and delicate things, before the Sisters could get their hands on them!

These private gifts were not the only nor the largest ones. The *Times,* which you will remember had been the first to reveal the terrible conditions in the Crimea, now set to work and organized a fund for the relief of the wounded. A subscription list was opened, and from every part of the United Kingdom money flowed in like water. The *Times* undertook to distribute the money, and appointed a good and wise man, Mr. McDonald, to go out to the East and see how it could best be applied.

And now a strange thing came to pass; the sort of thing that, in one way or another, was constantly happening in connection with the Crimean War. Mr. McDonald went to the highest authorities in the War Office and told of his purpose. They bowed and smiled and said the *Times* and its subscribers were very kind, but the fact was that such ample provision had been made by the Government that it was hardly likely the money would be needed. Mr. McDonald opened his eyes wide; but he was a wise man, as I have said; so he bowed and smiled in return, and going to Sidney Herbert, told his story to him.

"Go!" said Mr. Herbert; "Go out to the Crimea!" and he went.

When he reached the seat of war, it was the same thing over again. The high officials were very polite, very glad to see him, very pleased that the people of England were so sympathetic and patriotic; but the fact was that nothing was wanted; they were amply supplied; in short, everything was "all right."

Many men, after this second rebuff, would have given the matter up and gone home; but Mr. McDonald was not of that kind. While he was considering what step to take next, one man came forward to help him; one man who was brave enough to defy Red Tape, for the sake of his soldiers. This was the surgeon of the 39th regiment. I wish I knew his name, so that you and I could remember it. He came to Mr. McDonald and told him that his regiment, which had been stationed at Gibraltar, had been ordered to the Crimea and had now reached the Bosporus. They were going on to the Crimea, to pass the winter in bitter cold, amid ice and snow; and they had no clothes save the light linen suits which had been given them to wear under the hot sun of Gibraltar.

Here was a chance for the *Times* fund! Without more ado Mr. McDonald went into the bazaars of Constantinople and bought flannels and woolens, until every man in that regiment had a good warm winter suit in which to face the Crimean winter.

Did anyone else follow the example of the surgeon of the 39th? Not one! Probably many persons thought he had done a shocking thing, by thus exposing the lack of provision in the army for its soldiers' comfort. This was casting reflection upon Red Tape!

Better for the soldier to freeze and die, than for a slur to be cast upon those in authority, upon the rules of the service!

So, though McDonald stood with hands held out, as it were, offering help, no one came forward to take it.

He went to Scutari, and here at first it was the same thing. He offered his aid to the chief medical authority over the hospitals; the reply was calm and precise: "Nothing was wanted!" He went still higher, to "another and more august quarter"; the answer was still more emphatic: there was no possible occasion for help; soldiers and sailors had everything they required; if he wished to dispose of the *Times* fund, it might be a good thing to build an English church at Pera!

"Yet, at that very time," says the historian of the Crimea, "wants so dire as to include want of hospital furniture and of shirts for the patients, and of the commonest means for maintaining cleanliness, were afflicting our stricken soldiery in the hospitals."[6]

Mr. McDonald did not build an English church; instead, he went to the Barrack Hospital and asked for the Lady-in-Chief.

I should like to have seen Florence Nightingale's face when she heard his story. No help needed? The soldiers supplied with everything they needed? Everything "all right"?

"Come with me!" she said.

---

[6] Kinglake, "Invasion of the Crimea."

She took him through the wards of the Barrack Hospital, and showed him what had been done, and what an immense deal was yet to do; how, though many were comfortably clad, yet fresh hundreds were arriving constantly, half naked, without a shred of clean or decent clothing on their backs; how far the demand was beyond the supply; how fast her own stores were dwindling, and how many of the private offerings were unsuitable for the needs they were sent to fill; how many men were still, after all her labors, lying on the floor because there were not beds enough to go round.

All these things good Mr. McDonald saw, and laid to heart; but he saw other things besides.

Perhaps some of you have visited a hospital. You have seen the bright, fresh, pleasant rooms, the rows of snowy cots, the bright faces of the nurses, here and there flowers and pictures; seeing two or three hundred patients, it has seemed to you as if you had seen all the sick people in the world. Was it not so?

In the Barrack Hospital (and this, remember, was but one of eight, and these eight the English hospitals alone!) there were two or three thousand patients; it was a City of Pain. Its streets were long, narrow rooms or corridors, bare and gloomy; no furniture save the endless rows of cots and mattresses, "packed like sardines," as one eye-witness says; its citizens, men in every stage of sickness and suffering; some tossing in fever and delirium; some moaning in pain that even a soldier's strength could not bear silently; some ghastly with terrible wounds; some sinking into their final sleep.

Following the light, slight figure of his guide through these narrow streets of the City of Pain, McDonald saw and noted that

"Wherever there is disease in its most dangerous form, and the hand of the Spoiler distressingly nigh, there is this incomparable woman sure to be seen. Her benignant presence is an influence for good comfort even among the struggles of expiring nature. She is a 'ministering angel' without any exaggeration in these hospitals, and as the slender form glides quietly along each corridor, every poor fellow's face softens with gratitude at the sight of her. When all the medical officers have retired for the night, and silence and darkness have settled down upon those miles of prostrate sick, she may be observed alone, with lamp in her hand, making her solitary rounds.

"The popular instinct was not mistaken which, when she set out from England, hailed her as a heroine; I trust she may not earn her title to a higher though sadder appellation. No one who has observed her fragile figure and delicate health can avoid misgivings lest these should fail. . . . I confidently assert that but for Miss Nightingale the people of England would scarcely, with all their solicitude, have been spared the additional pang of knowing, which they must have done sooner or later, that their soldiers, even in the hospitals, had found scanty refuge and relief from the unparalleled miseries with which this war has hitherto been attended."

Look with me for a moment into one of these wards, these "miles of sick" through which the agent of the *Times* passed with his guide. It is night. Outside, the world is wide and wonderful with moon and stars. Beyond the dark-blue waters of the Bosporus, the lights of Stamboul flash and twinkle; nearer at hand, the moonlight falls on the white city of the dead, and shows its dark cypresses standing like silent guardians beside the marble tombs; nearer yet, it falls full on the bare, gaunt square of building that crowns the hill. The windows are narrow, but still the moonbeams struggle in, and cast a dim light along the corridor. The vaulted roof is lost in blackness; black, too, are the corners, and we cannot see where the orderly nods in his chair, or where the night nurse sits beside a dying patient. All is silent, save for a low moan or murmur from one cot or another. See where the moonbeam glimmers white on that cot under the window! That is where the Highland soldier is lying, he who came so near losing his arm the other day. The surgeons said it must be amputated, but the Lady-in-Chief begged for a little time. She thought that with care and nursing the arm might be saved; would they kindly delay the operation at least for a few days? The surgeons consented, for by this time no one could or would refuse her anything. The arm *was* saved; now the bones are knitting nicely, and by and by he will be well and strong again, with both arms to work and play and fight with.

But broken bones hurt even when they are knitting nicely, and the Highland lad cannot sleep; he lies tossing about on his narrow cot, gritting his teeth now and then as the pain bites, but still a happy and a thankful man. He stares about him through the gloom, trying to see who is awake and who asleep. But now he starts, for silently the door opens, and a tiny ray of light, like a golden finger, falls across his bed. A figure enters and closes the door softly; the figure of a woman, tall and slender, dressed in black, with white cap and apron. In her hand she carries a small shaded lamp. At sight of her the sick lad's eyes grow bright; he raises his sound arm and straightens the blanket, then waits in eager patience. Slowly the Lady with the Lamp draws near, stopping beside each cot, listening to the breathing and noting the color of the sleepers, whispering a word of cheer and encouragement to those who wake. Now she stands beside his bed, and her radiant smile is brighter, he thinks, than lamplight or moonlight. A few words in the low, musical voice, a pat to the bedclothes, a friendly nod, and she passes on to the next cot. As she goes, her shadow, hardly more noiseless than her footstep, falls across the sick man's pillow; he turns and kisses it, and then falls happily asleep.

So she comes and passes, like a light; and so her very shadow is blessed, and shall be blessed so long as memory endures.

CHAPTER XII

WINTER

O the long and dreary winter!
O the cold and cruel winter!
Ever thicker, thicker, thicker
Froze the ice on lake and river,
Ever deeper, deeper, deeper
Fell the snow o'er all the landscape,
Fell the covering snow, and drifted
Through the forest, round the village.

. . . . . .

O the famine and the fever!
O the wasting of the famine!
O the blasting of the fever!
O the wailing of the children!
O the anguish of the women!
All the earth was sick and famished;
Hungry was the air around them,
Hungry was the sky above them,
And the hungry stars in heaven
Like the eyes of wolves glared at them! [7]

[7] "Hiawatha," by Henry Wadsworth Longfellow.

HE bad weather commenced about November the 10th, and has continued ever since. A winter campaign is under no circumstances child's play; but here, where the troops had no cantonments to take shelter in, where large bodies were collected in one spot, and where the want of sufficient fuel soon made itself felt, it told with the greatest severity upon the health, not of the British alone, but of the French and Turkish troops. . . . To the severity of the winter the whole army can bear ample testimony. The troops have felt it in all its intensity; and when it is considered that they have been under canvas from ten to twelve months—that they had no other shelter from the sun in summer, and no other protection from wet and snow, cold and tempestuous winds, such as have scarcely been known even in this climate, in winter—and that they passed from a life of total inactivity, already assailed by deadly disease, to one of the greatest possible exertion—it cannot be a matter of surprise that a fearful sickness has prevailed throughout their ranks, and that the men still suffer from it."—Lord Raglan to Lord Panmure, February, 1855.

After the battle of Inkerman, the allied armies turned all their energies to the siege of Sebastopol, the principal city of the Crimea. You will read some day about this memorable siege, one of the most famous in history, and about the prodigies of valor performed by both besiegers and besieged; but I can only touch briefly on those aspects of it which are connected with my subject.

The winter of 1854–5 was, as Lord Raglan says, one of unexampled severity, even in that land of bitter winters. On November 14th a terrible hurricane swept the country, bringing death and ruin to Russians and allies alike. In Sebastopol itself trees were torn up by the roots, buildings unroofed, and much damage done; in the camps of the besiegers things were even worse. Tents were torn in shreds and swept away like dead leaves; not only the soldiers' tents, but the great hospital marquees were destroyed, and the sick and wounded left exposed to bitter blast and freezing sleet. The trenches were flooded; no fires could be lit, and therefore no food cooked; and when the snowstorm came which followed the tempest, many a brave fellow lay down famished and exhausted, and the white blanket covered his last sleep.

In the harbor even more ruin was wrought, for the ships were dashed about like broken toys that a wilful child flings hither and thither. The *Prince*, which had just arrived loaded with clothing, medicines, stores of every description, went down with all her precious freight; the *Resolute* was lost, too, the principal ammunition ship of the army; and other vessels loaded with hay for the horses, a supply which would have fed them for twenty days.

This dreadful calamity was followed by day after day of what the soldiers called "Inkerman weather," with heavy mists and low drizzling clouds; then came bitter, killing frost, then snow, thaw, sleet, frost again, and so round and round in a cruel circle; and through every variation of weather the soldier's bed was the earth, now deep in snow, now bare and hard as iron, now thick with nauseous mud. All day long the soldiers toiled in the trenches with pick and spade, often under fire, always on the alert; others on night duty, "five nights out of six, a large proportion of them constantly under fire."

Is it to be wondered at that plague and cholera broke out in the camp of the besiegers, and that a steady stream of poor wretches came creeping up the hill at Scutari?

The Lady-in-Chief was ready for them. Thanks to the *Times* fund and other subscriptions, she now had ample provision for many days. Moreover, by this winter time her influence so dominated the hospital that not only was there no opposition to her wishes, but everyone flew to carry them out. The rough orderlies, who had growled and sworn at the notion of a woman coming to order them about, were now her slaves. Her unvarying courtesy, her sweet and heavenly kindness, woke in many a rugged breast feelings of which it had never dreamed; and every man who worked for her was for the time at least a knight and a gentleman. It was bitter, hard work; she spared them no more than she spared herself; but they labored as no rules of the service had ever made them work. Through it all, not one of them, orderlies or common soldiers, ever failed her "in obedience, thoughtful attention, and considerate delicacy." "Never," she herself says, "came from any of them one word or one look which a gentleman would not have used; and while paying this humble tribute to humble courtesy, the tears come into my eyes as I think how amidst scenes of loathsome disease and death there arose above it all the innate dignity, gentleness and chivalry of the men (for never surely was chivalry so strikingly exemplified), shining in the midst of what must be considered as the lowest sinks of human misery, and preventing instinctively the use of one expression which could distress a gentlewoman."

If it was so with the orderlies, you can imagine how it was with the poor fellows for whom she was working. Every smile from her was a gift; every word was a precious treasure to be stored away and kept through life. They would do anything she asked, for they knew she would do anything in her power for them. When any specially painful operation was to be performed (there was not always chloroform enough, alas! and in any case it was not given so freely in those days as it is now), the Lady-in-Chief would come quietly into the operating room and take her stand beside the patient; and looking up into that calm, steadfast face, and meeting the tender gaze of those pitying eyes that never flinched from any sight of pain or horror, he would take courage and nerve himself to bear the pain, since she was there to help him bear it.

"We call her the Angel of the Crimea," one soldier wrote home. "Could bad men be bad in the presence of an angel? Impossible!"

Another wrote: "Before she came there was such cussin' and swearin' as you never heard; but after she came it was as holy as a church."

And still another—perhaps our Highland lad of the night vigil, perhaps another—wrote to his people: "She would speak to one and another, and nod and smile to many more; but she could not do it to all, you know, for we lay there by hundreds; but we could kiss her shadow as it fell, and lay our heads on our pillows again content."

Miss Nightingale never wearied of bearing testimony to the many virtues of the British soldier. She loved to tell stories like the following:

"I remember a sergeant who, on picket—the rest of the picket killed, and himself battered about the head—stumbled back to camp (before Sebastopol), and on his way picked up a wounded man and brought him on his shoulders to the lines, where he fell down insensible. When, after many hours, he recovered his senses, I believe after trepanning, his first words were to ask after his comrade: 'Is he alive?'

" 'Comrade indeed! yes, he's alive—it's the General!' At that moment the General, though badly wounded, appeared at the bedside. 'Oh! General, it was you, was it, I brought in? I'm so glad; I didn't know your honor. But if I'd known it was you, I'd have saved you all the same!' "

I must not leave the story of this winter without telling of all that Miss Nightingale did for the soldiers' wives. There were many of these poor women, who had come out to this far country to be near their husbands. There was no proper provision for them, and Miss Nightingale found them in a wretched condition, living in three or four damp, dark rooms in the basement of the hospital. Their clothes were worn out; they were barefooted and bareheaded. We are told that "the only privacy to be obtained was by hanging up rags of clothes on lines. There, by the light of a rush-light, the meals were taken, the sick attended, and there the babies were born and nourished. There were twenty-two babies born from November to December, and many more during the winter."[8]

The Lady-in-Chief soon put an end to this state of things. First she fed and clothed the women from her own stores, and saw that the little babies were made warm and comfortable. In January a fever broke out among the women, owing to a broken drain in the basement, and she found a house near by, had it cleaned and furnished, and persuaded the commandant to move the women into it. All through the winter she helped these poor souls in every way, employing some in the laundry, finding situations for others in Constantinople, sending widows home to England, helping to start a school for the children. Altogether about five hundred women were helped out of the miserable condition in which she found them, and were enabled to earn their own living honestly and respectably. Writing of these times later, Miss Nightingale says: "When the improvements in our system which the war must suggest are discussed, let not the wife and child of the soldier be forgotten."

Another helper came out to Scutari in those winter days; a gallant Frenchman, M. Soyer, who had been for years *chef* of one of the great London clubs, and who knew all that there was to know about cookery. He read the *Times*, and in February, 1855, he wrote to the editor:

---

[8] Tooley, "Life of Florence Nightingale," p. 154.

"SIR: After carefully perusing the letter of your correspondent, dated Scutari. . . . I perceive that, though the kitchen under the superintendence of Miss Nightingale affords so much relief, the system of management at the large one in the Barrack Hospital is far from being perfect. I propose offering my services gratuitously, and proceeding direct to Scutari at my own personal expense, to regulate that important department, if the Government will honor me with their confidence, and grant me the full power of acting according to my knowledge and experience in such matters."

It was April before M. Soyer reached Scutari. He went at once to the Barrack Hospital, asked for Miss Nightingale, and was received by her in her office, which he calls "a sanctuary of benevolence." They became friends at once, for each could help the other and greatly desired to do so.

"I must especially express my gratitude to Miss Nightingale," says the good gentleman in his record of the time, "who from her extraordinary intelligence and the good organization of her kitchen procured me every material for making a commencement, and thus saved me at least one week's sheer loss of time, as my model kitchen did not arrive until Saturday last."

M. Soyer, on his side, brought all kinds of things which Miss Nightingale rejoiced to see: new stoves, new kinds of fuel, new appliances of many kinds which, in the first months of her work, she could never have hoped to see. He was full of energy, of ingenuity, and a fine French gayety and enthusiasm which must have been delightful to all the brave and weary workers in the City of Pain. He went everywhere, saw and examined everything; and told of what he saw, in his own flowery, fiery way. He told among other things how, coming back one night from a gay evening in the doctors' quarters, he was making his way through the hospital wards to his own room, when, as he turned the corner of a corridor, he came upon a scene which made him stop and hold his breath. At the foot of one cot stood a nurse, holding a lighted lamp. Its light fell on the sick man, who lay propped on pillows, gasping for breath, and evidently near his end. He was speaking, in hoarse and broken murmurs; sitting beside him, bending near to catch the painful utterances, was the Lady-in-Chief, pencil and paper in hand, writing down the words as he spoke them. Now the dying man fumbled beneath his pillow, brought out a watch and some other small objects, and laid them in her hand; then with a sigh of relief, sank back content. It was two o'clock. Miss Nightingale had been on her feet, very likely, the whole day, perhaps had not even closed her eyes in sleep; but word was brought to her that this man was given up by the doctors, and had only a few hours to live; and in a moment she was by his side, to speak some final words of comfort, and to take down his parting message to wife and children.

The kind-hearted Frenchman never forgot this sight, yet it was one that might be seen any night in the Barrack Hospital. No man should die alone and uncomforted if Florence Nightingale and her women could help it.

This is how M. Soyer describes our heroine:

"She is rather high in stature, fair in complexion and slim in person; her hair is brown, and is worn quite plain; her physiognomy is most pleasing; her eyes, of a bluish tint, speak volumes, and are always sparkling with intelligence; her mouth is small and well formed, while her lips act in unison, and make known the impression of her heart—one seems the reflex of the other. Her visage, as regards expression, is very remarkable, and one can almost anticipate by her countenance what she is about to say; alternately, with matters of the most grave import, a gentle smile passes radiantly over her countenance, thus proving her evenness of temper; at other times, when wit or a pleasantry prevails, the heroine is lost in the happy, good-natured smile which pervades her face, and you recognize only the charming woman.

"Her dress is generally of a grayish or black tint; she wears a simple white cap, and often a rough apron. In a word, her whole appearance is religiously simple and unsophisticated. In conversation no member of the fair sex can be more amiable and gentle than Miss Nightingale. Removed from her arduous and cavalier-like duties, which require the nerve of a Hercules—and she possesses it when required—she is Rachel[9] on the stage in both tragedy and comedy."

The long and dreary winter was over. The snow was gone, and the birds sang once more among the cypresses of Scutari, and sunned themselves, and

[9] Rachel was a famous French actress, but I cannot imagine any real resemblance between her and Miss Nightingale.

bathed and splashed in the marble basins at the foot of the tombs; but there was no abatement of the stream that crept up the hill to the hospital. No frostbite now—I haven't told you about that, because it is too dreadful for me to tell or for you to hear—but no less sickness. Cholera was raging in the camp before Sebastopol, and typhus, and dysentery; the men were dying like flies. The dreaded typhus crept into the hospital and attacked the workers. Eight of the doctors were stricken down, seven of whom died. "For a time there was only one medical attendant in a fit state of health to wait on the sick in the Barrack Hospital, and his services were needed in twenty-four wards."

Next three of the devoted nurses were taken, two dying of fever, the third of cholera. More and more severe grew the strain of work and anxiety for Miss Nightingale, and those who watched her with loving anxiety trembled. So fragile, so worn; such a tremendous weight of care and responsibility on those delicate shoulders! Is she not paler than usual to-day? What would become of us if she—

Their fears were groundless; the time was not yet. Tending the dying physicians as she had tended their patients; walking, sad but steadfast, behind the bier that bore her dear and devoted helpers to the grave; adding each new burden to the rest, and carrying all with unbroken calm, unwearying patience; Florence Nightingale seemed to bear a charmed life. There is no record of any single instance, through that terrible winter and spring, of her being unable to perform the duties she had taken upon her. She might have said with Sir Galahad:

"My strength is as the strength of ten
Because my heart is pure."

CHAPTER XIII

MISS NIGHTINGALE
UNDER FIRE

I N May, 1855, Miss Nightingale decided to go to the Crimea, to inspect the hospitals there. In the six months spent at Scutari, she had brought its hospitals into excellent condition; now she felt that she must see what was being done and what still needed to be done elsewhere. Accordingly she set sail in the ship *Robert Lowe*, accompanied by her faithful friend Mr. Bracebridge, who, with his admirable wife, had come out with her from England, and had been her constant helper and adviser; M. Soyer, who was going to see how kitchen matters were going *là-bas*, and her devoted boy Thomas. Thomas had been a drummer boy. He was twelve years old, and devoted to his drum until he came under the spell of the Lady-in-Chief. Then he transferred his devotion to her, and became her aide-de-camp, following her wherever she went, and ready at any moment to give his life for her.

It was fair spring weather now, and the fresh, soft air and beautiful scenery must have been specially delightful to the women who had spent six months within the four bare walls of the hospital surrounded by misery and death; but when she found that there were some sick soldiers on board, Miss Nightingale begged to be taken to them. She went from one to another in her cheerful way, and every man felt better at once. Presently she came to a fever patient who was looking very discontented.

"This man will not take his medicine!" said the attendant.

"Why will you not take it?" asked Miss Nightingale, with her winning smile.

"Because I took some once," said the man, "and it made me sick, and I haven't liked physic ever since."

"But if I give it to you myself you will take it, won't you?"

I wonder if anyone ever refused Miss Nightingale anything!

"It will make me sick just the same, ma'am!" murmured the poor soul piteously; but he took the medicine, and forgot to be sick as she sat beside him and asked about the battle in which he had been wounded.

When they entered the harbor of Balaklava, they found all the vessels crowded with people. Word had got abroad that the Lady-in-Chief was expected, and everybody was agog to see the wonderful woman who had done such a great work in the hospitals of Scutari. The vessel was no sooner brought to anchor than all the doctors and officials of Balaklava came on board, eager to pay their respects and welcome her to their shore. For an hour she received these various guests, but she could not wait longer, and by the time Lord Raglan, the Commander-in-Chief, reached the vessel on the same errand, she had already begun her inspection of the hospital on shore. She never had any time to waste, and so she never lost any.

But the visit of a Commander-in-Chief must be returned; so the next day Miss Nightingale set out on horseback, with a party of friends, for the camp of the besiegers. M. Soyer, who was of the party, tells us that she "was attired simply in a genteel amazone, or riding-habit, and had quite a martial air. She was mounted upon a very pretty mare, of a golden color, which, by its gambols and caracoling, seemed proud to carry its noble charge. The weather was very fine. Our cavalcade produced an extraordinary effect upon the motley crowd of all nations assembled at Balaklava, who were astonished at seeing a lady so well escorted."

The road was very bad, and crowded with people of every nationality, riding horses, mules and asses, driving oxen and cows and sheep. Now they passed a cannon, stuck in the mud, its escort prancing and yelling around it; now a wagon overturned, its contents scattered on the road, its owner sitting on the ground lamenting. Everywhere horses were kicking and whinnying, men shouting and screaming. It is no wonder that Miss Nightingale's pretty mare "of a golden color" got excited too, and kicked and pranced with the rest; but her rider had not scampered over English downs and jumped English fences for nothing, and the pretty creature soon found that she, like everyone else, must obey the Lady-in-Chief.

The first hospital they came to was in the village of Kadikoi. After inspecting it, and seeing what was needed, Miss Nightingale and her party rode to the top of a hill near by; and here for the first time she looked down on the actual face of war; saw the white tents of the besiegers and in the distance the grim walls of the beleaguered city; saw, too, the puffs of white smoke from trench and bastion, heard the roar of cannon and the crackle of musketry. To the boy beside her no doubt it was a splendid and inspiring sight; but Florence Nightingale knew too well what it all meant, and turned away with a heavy heart.

Lord Raglan, not having been warned of her coming, was away; so, after visiting several small regimental hospitals, Miss Nightingale went on to the General Hospital before Sebastopol. Here she found some hundreds of sick and wounded. Word passed along the rows of cots that the "good lady of Scutari" was coming to visit them, and everywhere she was greeted with beaming smiles and murmurs of greeting and welcome. But when she came out again, and passed along toward the cooking encampment, she was recognized by some former patients of hers at the Barrack Hospital, and a great shout of rejoicing went up; a shout so loud that the golden mare capered again, and again had to learn who her mistress was.

Now they approached the walls of Sebastopol; and Miss Nightingale, who did not know what fear was, insisted upon having a nearer view of the city. They came to a point from which it could be conveniently seen; but here a sentry met them, and with a face of alarm begged them to dismount. "Sharp firing going

103

on here," he said, and he pointed to the fragments of shell lying about; "you'll be sure to attract attention, and they'll fire at you."

Miss Nightingale laughed at his fears, but consented to take shelter behind a stone redoubt, from which, with the aid of a telescope, she had a good view of the city.

But this was not enough. She must go into the trenches themselves. The sentry was horrified. "Madam," said he, " if anything happens I call upon these gentlemen to witness that I did not fail to warn you of the danger."

"My good young man," replied Miss Nightingale, "more dead and wounded have passed through my hands than I hope you will ever see in the battlefield during the whole of your military career; believe me, I have no fear of death."

They went on, and soon reached the Three-Mortar Battery, situated among the trenches and very near the walls. And here M. Soyer had a great idea, which he carried out to his immense satisfaction. You shall hear about it in his own words

"Before leaving the battery, I begged Miss Nightingale as a favor to give me her hand, which she did. I then requested her to ascend the stone rampart next the wooden gun carriage, and lastly to sit upon the centre mortar, to which requests she very gracefully and kindly acceded. 'Gentlemen,' I cried, 'behold this amiable lady sitting fearlessly upon that terrible instrument of war! Behold the heroic daughter of England—the soldier's friend!' All present shouted

104

'Bravo! hurrah! hurrah! Long live the daughter of England!' "

When Lord Raglan heard of this, he said that the "instrument of war" on which she sat ought to be called "the Nightingale mortar."

The 39th regiment was stationed close by; and seeing a lady—a strange enough sight in that place—seated on a mortar, gazing calmly about her, as if all her life had been spent in the trenches, the soldiers looked closer, and all at once recognized the beloved Lady-in-Chief, the Angel of the Crimea. They set up a shout that went ringing over the fields and trenches, and startled the Russians behind the walls of Sebastopol; and Miss Nightingale, startled too, but greatly touched and moved, came down from her mortar and mounted her horse to ride back to Balaklava.

It was a rough and fatiguing ride, and the next day she felt very tired; but she was used to being tired, and never thought much of it; so she set out to visit the General Hospital again. After spending several hours there, she went on to the Sanatorium, a collection of huts high up on a mountainside, nearly eight hundred feet above the sea. The sun was intensely hot, the ride a hard one; yet she not only reached it this day, but went up again the day after, to install three much-needed nurses there; this done, she went on with her work in the hospitals of Balaklava. But, alas! this time she had gone beyond even her strength. She was stricken down suddenly, in the midst of her work, with the worst form of Crimean fever.

The doctors ordered that she should be taken to the Sanatorium. Amid general grief and consternation she was laid on a stretcher, and the soldiers for whom she had so often risked her life bore her sadly through the streets of Balaklava and up the mountainside. A nurse went with her, a friend held a white umbrella between her and the pitiless sun, and poor little Thomas, "Miss Nightingale's man" as he had proudly called himself, followed the stretcher, crying bitterly. Indeed, it seemed as if everyone were crying. The rough soldiers—only she never found them rough—wept like children. It was a sad little procession that wound its way up the height, to the hut that had been set apart for the beloved sufferer. It was a neat, airy cabin, set on the banks of a clear stream. All about were spring buds and blossoms, and green, whispering trees; it was just such a place as she would have chosen for one of her own patients; and here, for several days, she lay between life and death.

The news spread everywhere; Florence Nightingale was ill—was dying! All Balaklava knew it; soon the tidings came to Scutari, to her own hospital, and the sick men turned their faces to the wall and wept, and longed to give their own lives for hers, if only that might be. The news came to England, and men looked and spoke—ay, and felt—as if some great national calamity threatened. But soon the messages changed their tone. The disease was checked; she was better; she was actually recovering, and would soon be well. Then all the Crimea rejoiced, and at Scutari they felt that spring had come indeed.

While she still lay desperately ill, a visitor climbed the rugged height to the Sanatorium, and knocked at the door of the little lonely hut. I think you must hear about this visit from Mrs. Roberts, the nurse who told M. Soyer about it.

"It was about five o'clock in the afternoon when he came. Miss Nightingale was dozing, after a very restless night. We had a storm that day, and it was very wet. I was in my room sewing when two men on horseback, wrapped in large guttapercha cloaks and dripping wet, knocked at the door. I went out, and one inquired in which hut Miss Nightingale resided.

"He spoke so loud that I said: 'Hist! hist! don't make such a horrible noise as that, my man,' at the same time making a sign with both hands for him to be quiet. He then repeated his question, but not in so loud a tone. I told him this was the hut.

" 'All right,' said he, jumping from his horse; and he was walking straight in when I pushed him back, asking what he meant and whom he wanted.

" 'Miss Nightingale,' said he.

" 'And pray who are you?'

" 'Oh, only a soldier,' was the reply, 'but I must see her—I have come a long way—my name is Raglan—she knows me very well.'

"Miss Nightingale overhearing him, called me in, saying: 'Oh! Mrs. Roberts, it is Lord Raglan. Pray tell him I have a very bad fever, and it will be dangerous for him to come near me.'

" 'I have no fear of fever or anything else,' said Lord Raglan.

"And before I had time to turn round, in came his lordship. He took up a stool, sat down at the foot of the bed, and kindly asked Miss Nightingale how she was, expressing his sorrow at her illness, and praising her for the good she had done for the troops. He wished her a speedy recovery, and hoped she might be able to continue her charitable and invaluable exertions, so highly appreciated by everyone, as well as by himself. He then bade Miss Nightingale goodbye, and went away. . . ."

After twelve days Miss Nightingale was pronounced convalescent. The doctors now earnestly begged her to return to England, telling her that her health absolutely required a long rest, with entire freedom from care. But she shook her head resolutely. Her work was not yet over; she would not desert her post. Weak as she was, she insisted on being taken back to Scutari; she would come back by and by, she said, and finish the work in the Crimea itself. Sick or well, there was no resisting the Lady-in-Chief. The stretcher was brought again, and eight soldiers carried her down the mountainside and so down to the port of Balaklava. The *Jura* lay at the wharf; a tackle was rigged, and the stretcher hoisted on board, the patient lying motionless but undaunted the while; but this vessel proved unsuitable, and she had to be moved twice before she was finally established on a private yacht, the *New London*.

Before she sailed, Lord Raglan came to see her again. It was the last time they ever met, for a few

weeks after the brave commander died, worn out by
the struggles and privations of the war, and—some
thought—broken-hearted by the disastrous repulse of
the British troops at the Redan.

Rather more than a month after she had left for
the Crimea, Miss Nightingale saw once more the towers and minarets of Constantinople flashing across the
Black-Sea water, and, on the other side of the narrow
Bosporus, the gaunt white walls which had come to
seem almost homelike to her. She was glad to get back
to her Scutari and her people. She knew she should get
well here, and so she did.

The welcome she received was most touching.
All the great people, commanders and high authorities,
met her at the pier, and offered her their houses, their
carriages, everything they had, to help her back to
strength; but far dearer to her than this were the
glances of weary eyes that brightened at her coming,
the waving of feeble hands, the cheers of feeble voices,
from the invalid soldiers who, like herself, were creeping back from death to life, and who felt, very likely,
that their chance of full recovery was a far better one
now that their angel had come back to dwell among
them.

As strength returned, Miss Nightingale loved to
walk in the great burying ground of which I have told
you; to rest under the cypress trees, and watch the little
birds, and pick wild flowers in that lovely, lonely place.
There are strange stories about the birds of Scutari, by
the way; the Turks believe that they are the souls of
sinners, forced to flit and hover forever, without rest;

but it is not likely that thoughts of this kind troubled Miss Nightingale, as she watched the pretty creatures taking their bath, or pecking at the crumbs she scattered.

Birds and flowers, green trees and soft, sweet air—all these things ministered to her, and helped her on the upward road to health and strength; and before long she was able to take up again the work which she loved, and which was waiting for her hand.

CHAPTER XIV

THE CLOSE OF THE WAR

THE sun soared over the gulf, where the water, covered with ships at anchor, and with sail- and row-boats in motion, played merrily in its warm and luminous rays. A light breeze, which scarcely shook the leaves of the stunted oak bushes that grew beside the signal station, filled the sails of the boats, and made the waves ripple softly. On the other side of the gulf Sebastopol was visible, unchanged, with its unfinished church, its column, its quay, the boulevard which cut the hill with a green band, the elegant library building, its little lakes of azure blue, with their forests of masts, its picturesque aqueducts, and, above all that, clouds of a bluish tint, formed by powder smoke, lighted up from time to time by the red flame of the firing. It was the same proud and beauti- ful Sebastopol, with its festal air, surrounded on one side by the yellow smoke-crowned hills, on the other by the sea, deep blue in color and sparkling brilliantly in the sun. At the horizon, where the smoke of a steamer traced a black line, white, narrow clouds were rising, precursors of a wind. Along the whole line of the fortifications, along the heights, especially on the left side, spurted out suddenly, torn by a visible flash, although it was broad daylight, plumes of thick white smoke, which, assuming various forms, extended, rose, and colored the sky with sombre tints. These jets of smoke came out on all sides—from the hills, from the hostile batteries, from the city—and flew toward the sky. The noise of the explosions shook the air with a continuous roar. Toward noon these smoke puffs became rarer and rarer, and the vibrations of the air strata became less frequent.

" 'Do you know that the second bastion is no longer replying?' said the hussar officer on horseback, 'it is entirely demolished. It is terrible!'

" 'Yes, and the Malakoff replies twice out of three times,' answered the one who was looking through the field-glass. 'This silence is driving me mad! They are firing straight on the Korniloff battery and that is not replying.'

" 'There is a movement in the trenches; they are marching in close columns.'

" 'Yes, I see it well,' said one of the sailors; 'they are advancing by columns. We must set the signal.'

" 'But see, there—see! They are coming out of the trenches!'

"They could see, in fact, with the naked eye black spots going down from the hill into the ravine, and proceeding from the French batteries toward our bastions. In the foreground, in front of the former, black spots could be seen very near our lines. Suddenly, from different points of the bastion at the same time, spurted out the white plumes of the discharges, and, thanks to the wind, the noise of a lively fusillade could be heard, like the patter of a heavy rain against the windows. The black lines advanced, wrapped in a curtain of smoke, and came nearer. The fusillade increased in violence. The smoke burst out at shorter and shorter intervals, extended rapidly along the line in a single light, lilac-colored cloud, unrolling and enlarging itself by turns, furrowed here and there by flashes or rent by black points. All the noises mingled together in the tumult of one continued roar.

" 'It is an assault,' said the officer, pale with emotion, handing his glass to the sailor.

"Cossacks and officers on horseback went along the road, preceding the commander-in-chief in his carriage, accompanied by his suite. Their faces expressed the painful emotion of expectation.

" 'It is impossible that it is taken!' said the officer on horseback.

" 'God in heaven—the flag! Look now!' cried the other, choked by emotion, turning away from the glass. 'The French flag is in the Malakoff mamelon!' "

It is thus that Tolstoi, the great Russian writer, describes the fall of Sebastopol, as he saw it. At the same moment that the French were taking the Malakoff redoubt, the British were storming the Redan, from which they had been so disastrously repulsed three months before. The flags of the allied armies floated over both forts, and in the night that followed the Russians marched silently out of the fallen city, leaving flames and desolation behind them.

The war was over. The good news sped to England, and the great guns of the Tower of London thundered out "Victory!"

"Victory!" answered every arsenal the country over. "Victory!" rang the bells in every village steeple. "Victory!" cried man, woman, and child throughout the length and breadth of the land. But mingled with the shouts of rejoicing was a deeper note, one of thankfulness that the cruel war was done, and peace come at last.

In these happy days Miss Nightingale's name was on all lips. What did not England owe to her, the heroic woman who had offered her life, and had all but lost it, for the soldiers of her country? What should England do to show her gratitude? People were on fire to do something, make some return to Florence Nightingale for her devoted services. From the Queen to the cottager, all were asking: "What shall we do for her?"

It was decided to consult her friends, the Sidney Herberts, as to the shape that a testimonial of the country's love and gratitude should take in order to be acceptable to Miss Nightingale. Mrs. Herbert, being asked, replied: "There is but one testimonial which would be accepted by Miss Nightingale. The one wish of her heart has long been to found a hospital in London and to work it on her own system of unpaid nursing, and I have suggested to all who have asked my advice in this matter to pay any sums that they may feel disposed to give, or that they may be able to collect, into Messrs. Coutts' Bank, where a subscription list for the purpose is about to be opened, to be called the 'Nightingale Hospital Fund,' the sum subscribed to be presented to her on her return home, which will enable her to carry out her object regarding the reform of the nursing system in England."

Here was something definite indeed. A committee was instantly formed—a wonderful committee, with "three dukes, nine other noblemen, the Lord Mayor, two judges, five right honorables, foremost naval and military officers, physicians, lawyers, London aldermen, dignitaries of the Church, dignitaries of nonconformist churches, twenty members of Parliament, and several eminent men of letters";[10] and the subscription was opened. How the money came pouring in! You would think no one had ever spent money before. The rich gave their thousands, the poor their pennies. There were fairs and concerts and entertainments of every description, to swell the Nightingale fund; but the offering that must have touched Miss Nightingale's heart most deeply was that of the soldiers and sailors of England. "The officers and men of nearly every regiment and many of the vessels contributed a day's pay."[11] That meant more to her, I warrant, than any rich man's thousands.

Before a year had passed, the fund amounted to over forty thousand pounds; and there is no knowing how much higher it might have gone had not Miss Nightingale herself come home and stopped it.

[10] Tooley, "Life of Florence Nightingale," p. 220.
[11] Tooley, "Life of Florence Nightingale," p. 223.

That was enough, she said; if they wanted to give more money, they might give it to the sufferers from the floods in France.

But she did not come home at once; no indeed! The war might be over, but her work was not, and she would never leave it while anything remained undone. The war was over, but the hospitals, especially those of the Crimea itself, were still filled with sick and wounded soldiers, and until the formal peace was signed an "army of occupation" must still remain in the Crimea. Miss Nightingale knew well that idleness is the worst possible thing for soldiers (as for everyone); and while she cared for the sick and wounded, she took as much pains to provide employment and amusement for the rest. As soon as she had fully regained her strength, she returned to the Crimea as she had promised to do, set up two new camp hospitals, and established a staff of nurses, taking the charge of the whole nursing department upon herself. These new hospitals were on the heights above Balaklava, not far from where she had passed the days of her own desperate illness. She established herself in a hut close by the hospitals and the Sanatorium, and here she spent a second winter of hard work and exposure. It was bitter cold up there on the mountainside. The hut was not weather-proof, and they sometimes found their beds covered with snow in the morning; but they did not mind trifles like this.

"The sisters are all quite well and cheerful," writes Miss Nightingale; "thank God for it! They have made their hut look quite tidy, and put up with the cold and inconveniences with the utmost self-abnegation. Everything, even the ink, freezes in our hut every night."

In all weathers she rode or drove over the rough and perilous roads, often at great risk of life and limb. Her carriage being upset one day, and she and her attendant nurse injured, a friend had a carriage made on purpose for her, to be at once secure and comfortable.

It was "composed of wood battens framed on the outside and basketwork. In the interior it is lined with a sort of waterproof canvas. It has a fixed head on the hind part and a canopy running the full length, with curtains at the side to inclose the interior. The front driving seat removes, and thus the whole forms a sort of small tilted wagon with a welted frame, suspended on the back part on which to recline, and well padded round the sides. It is fitted with patent breaks to the hind wheels so as to let it go gently down the steep hills of the Turkish roads."[12]

This curious carriage is still preserved at Lea Hurst. Miss Nightingale left it behind her when she returned to England, and it was about to be sold, with other abandoned articles, when our good friend M. Soyer heard of it; he instantly bought it, sent it to England, and afterwards had the pleasure of restoring it to its owner. She must have been amused, I think, but no doubt she was pleased, too, at the kindly thought.

But this comfortable carriage only increased her labors, in one way, for with it she went about more than ever. No weather was too severe, no snowstorm

---

[12] Tooley, "Life of Florence Nightingale," p. 229.

too furious, to keep her indoors; the men needed her and she must go to them. "She was known to stand for hours at the top of a bleak rocky mountain near the hospitals, giving her instructions while the snow was falling heavily. Then in the bleak dark night she would return down the perilous mountain road with no escort save the driver."[13]

It was not only for the invalids that Miss Nightingale toiled through this second winter; much of her time was given to the convalescents and those who were on active duty. She established libraries, and little "reading huts," where the men could come and find the English magazines and papers, and a stock of cheerful, entertaining books, carefully chosen by the dear lady who knew so well what they liked. She got up lectures, too, and classes for those who wished to study this or that branch of learning; and she helped to establish a café at Inkerman, where the men could get hot coffee and chocolate and the like in the bitter winter weather. There really seems no end to the good and kind and lovely things she did. I must not forget one thing, which may seem small to some of you, but which was truly great in the amount of good that came from it. Ever since she first came out to Scutari, she had used all her influence to persuade the soldiers to write home regularly to their families. The sick lads in the hospital learned that if they would write a letter—just two or three lines, to tell mother or sister that they were alive and doing well—and would send it to the Lady-in-Chief, she would put a stamp on it and speed it on its way. So now, in all the little libraries and read-

[13] Tooley, "Life of Florence Nightingale," p. 231–32.

ing huts, there were pens, ink and paper, envelopes and stamps; and when Miss Nightingale looked in at one of these cheerful little gathering places, we may be sure that she asked Jim or Joe whether he had written to his mother this week, and bade him be sure not to forget it. Does this seem to you a small thing? Wait till you go away from home, and see what the letters that come from home mean to you; then multiply that by ten, and you will know partly, but not entirely, what your letters mean to those at home. It has always seemed to me that this was a very bright star in Miss Nightingale's crown of glory.

The soldier's wife and child, mother and sister, were always in her thoughts. Not only did she persuade the men to write home, but she used all her great influence to induce them to send home their pay to their families. At Scutari she had a money-order office of her own, and four afternoons in each month she devoted to receiving money from the soldiers who brought it to her, and forwarding it to England. It is estimated that about a thousand pounds was sent each month, in small sums of twenty or thirty shillings. "This money," says Miss Nightingale, "was literally so much rescued from the canteen and drunkenness."

After the fall of Sebastopol the British Government followed her example, and set up money-order offices in several places, with excellent results.

Sometimes it was Miss Nightingale herself who wrote home to the soldier's family; sad, sweet letters, telling how the husband or father had done his duty gallantly, and had died as a brave man should; giving his last messages, and inclosing the mementos he had left for them. To many a humble home these letters brought comfort and support in the hour of trial, and were treasured—are no doubt treasured to this day— like the relics of a blessed saint.

The Treaty of Peace was signed at Paris on March 30, 1856, and now all hearts in the Crimea turned toward home. One by one the hospitals were closed, as their inmates recovered strength; one by one the troopships were filled with soldiers—ragged, gaunt, hollow-eyed, yet gay and light-hearted as schoolboys—and started on the homeward voyage; yet still the Lady-in-Chief lingered. Not while one sick man remained would Florence Nightingale leave her post. Indeed, at the last moment she found a task that none but herself might have taken up. The troopships were gone; but here, on the camping ground before Sebastopol, were fifty or sixty poor women, left behind when their husbands' regiments had sailed, helpless and—I was going to say friendless, but nothing could be more untrue; for they gathered in their distress round the hut of the Lady-in-Chief, imploring her aid; and she soon had them on board a British ship, speeding home after the rest.

And now the end had come, and there was only one more thing to do, one more order to give; the result of that last order is seen to-day by all who visit that far-away land of the Crimea. On the mountain heights above Balaklava, on a peak not far from the Sanatorium where she labored and suffered, towers a great cross of white marble, shining like snow against the deep blue sky. This is the "Nightingale Cross," her own tribute to the brave men and the devoted nurses who died in the war. At the foot of the cross are these words

"Lord have mercy upon us."

To every Englishman—nay, to everyone of any race who loves noble thoughts and noble deeds—this monument will always be a sacred and a venerable one.

In the spring of this year, Lord Ellesmere, speaking before Parliament, said:

"My Lords, the agony of that time has become a matter of history. The vegetation of two successive springs has obscured the vestiges of Balaklava and of Inkerman. Strong voices now answer to the roll call, and sturdy forms now cluster round the colors. The ranks are full, the hospitals are empty. The angel of mercy still lingers to the last on the scene of her labors; but her mission is all but accomplished. Those long arcades of Scutari, in which dying men sat up to catch the sound of her footstep or the flutter of her dress, and fell back on the pillow content to have seen her shadow as it passed, are now comparatively deserted. She may be thinking how to escape, as best she may, on her return, the demonstration of a nation's appreciation of the deeds and motives of Florence Nightingale."

This was precisely what the Lady-in-Chief was thinking. She meant to return to England as quietly as she left it; and she succeeded. The British Government begged her to accept a man-of-war as her own for the time being; she was much obliged, but would rather not. She went over to Scutari, saw the final closing of the hospitals there, and took a silent farewell of that place of many memories; then stepped quietly on board a French vessel, and sailed for France. A few days later—so the story goes—a lady quietly dressed in black, and closely veiled, entered the back door of Lea Hurst. The old butler saw the intruder, and hastened forward to stop her way—and it was "Miss Florence!"

CHAPTER XV

THE TASKS OF PEACE

NOW, the people of England had been on tiptoe for some days with eagerness, waiting to welcome the heroine of the Crimea back to her native shores. They would give her such a reception as no one had ever yet had in that land of hospitality and welcomings. She should have bells and cannon and bonfires, processions and deputations and addresses—she should have everything that anybody could think of.

When they found that their heroine had slipped quietly through their fingers, as it were, and was back in her own peaceful home once more, people were sadly disappointed. They must give up the cannon and the bonfires; but at least they might have a glimpse of her! So hundreds of people crowded the roads and lanes about Lea Hurst, waiting and watching. An old lady living at the park gate told Mrs. Tooley: "I remember the crowds as if it was yesterday. It took me all my time to answer them. Folks came in carriages and on foot, and there was titled people among them, and a lot of soldiers, some of them without arms and legs, who had been nursed by Miss Florence in the hospital, and I remember one man who had been shot through both eyes coming and asking to see Miss Florence. But not ten out of the hundreds who came got a glimpse of her. If they wanted help about their pensions, they were told to put it down in writing, and Miss Florence's maid came with an answer. Of course she was willing to help everybody, but it stood to reason she could not receive them all; why, the park wouldn't have held all the folks that came, and besides, the old Squire wouldn't have his daughter made a staring stock of."[14]

After the first disappointment—which after all was perfectly natural—all sensible people realized how weary Miss Nightingale must be after her tremendous labors, and how much she must need rest. All who knew her, too, knew that she never could abide public "demonstrations"; so they left her in peace, and began sending her things, to show their gratitude in a different way. The first gift of this kind she had received before she left the Crimea, from good Queen Victoria herself. This was "the Nightingale Jewel," as it is called; "a ruby-red enamel cross on a white field, encircled by a black band with the words: 'Blessed are the merciful.' The letters V. R.; surmounted by a crown in diamonds, are impressed upon the centre of the cross. Green enamel branches of palm, tipped with gold, form the framework of the shield, while around their stems is a riband of blue enamel, with the single word 'Crimea.' On the top are three brilliant stars of diamonds. On the back is an inscription written by the Queen."

[14] Tooley, "Life of Florence Nightingale," p. 240.

Another gift received on the scene of her labors was a magnificent diamond bracelet sent her by the Sultan of Turkey.

I do not know of any more jewels; but two gifts that Miss Nightingale prized highly were a fine case of cutlery sent her by the workmen of Sheffield, each knife blade inscribed with the words "Presented to Florence Nightingale, 1857," and the silver-bound oak case inlaid with a representation of the Good Samaritan; and a beautiful pearl-inlaid writing desk, presented by her friends and neighbors near Lea Hurst.

All these things were very touching; still more touching were the letters that came from all over the country, thanking and blessing her for all she had done. Truly it was a happy home coming.

Miss Nightingale knew that she was very, very weary; she realized that she must have a long rest, but she little thought how long it must be. She, and all her friends, thought that after a few months she would be able to take up again the work she so loved, and become the active leader in introducing the new methods of nursing into England. But the months passed, and grew from few to many, and still her strength did not return. The next year, indeed, when the dreadful Indian Mutiny broke out, she wrote to her friend Lady Canning, wife of the Governor-General of India, offering to come at twenty-four hours' notice "if there was anything to do in her line of business"; but Lady Canning knew that she was not equal to such a task.

Slowly, gradually, the truth came to Florence Nightingale: she was never going to be strong or well again. Always delicate, the tremendous labors of the Crimea had been too much for her. While the work went on, the frail body answered the call of the powerful will, the undaunted mind, the great heart; now that the task was finished, it sank down broken and exhausted. Truly, she had given her life, as much as any soldier who fought and died in the trenches or on the battlefield.

And what did she do when she finally came to realize this? Did she give up, and say, "My work on earth is done?" Not she! There may have been some dark hours, but the world has never heard of them. She never for an instant thought of giving up her work; she simply changed the methods of it. The poor tired body must stay in bed or on the sofa; very well! But the mind was not tired at all; the will was not weakened; the heart had not ceased to throb with love and compassion for the sick, the sorrowful, the suffering; the question was to find the way in which they could work with as little trouble as might be to their poor sick friend the body.

The way was soon found. Whether at Lea Hurst or in London (for she now spent a good deal of time in the great city, to be near the centre of things), her sick room became one of the busiest places in all England.

Schemes for army reform, for hospital reform, for reform in everything connected with the poor and the sick—all these must be brought to Miss Nightingale. All the soldiers in the country must write to her whenever they wanted anything, from a pension down to a wooden leg (to their honor be it said, however, that though she was overwhelmed with begging letters from all parts of the country, not a soldier ever asked her for money). The Nightingale fund, now nearly fifty thousand pounds, was administered under her advice and direction, and the first Training School for Nurses organized and opened. The old incapable, ignorant nurse vanished, and the modern nurse, educated, methodical, clear-eyed and clear-headed, took her place quietly; one of the great changes of modern times was effected, and the hand that directed it was the same one that we have seen holding the lamp, or writing down the dying soldier's last words, in the Barrack Hospital at Scutari.

That slender hand wrote books with all the rest of its work. In the sick room as in the hospital, Miss Nightingale had no time to waste. Her "Hospital Notes" may be read to-day with the keenest interest by all who care to know more of that great story of the Crimean War; her "Notes on Nursing" became the handbook of the Nursing Reform, and ought to be in the hands of every nurse to-day as it was in 1860, when it was written. Nor in the hands of nurses only; I wish every girl and every boy who reads this story would try to find that slender, dingy volume in some library, and "read, mark, learn, and inwardly digest" its contents. They would know a good deal more than they do now. Well might Miss Nightingale write, in 1861: "I have passed the last four years between four walls, only varied to other four walls once a year; and I believe there is no prospect but of my health becoming ever worse and worse till the hour of my release. But I have never ceased, during one waking hour since my return to England five years ago, laboring for the welfare of the army at home, as I did abroad, and no hour have I given to friendship or amusement during that time, but all to work."

Drop a stone in the water and see how the circles spread, growing wider and wider. After a while you cannot see them, but you know that the motion you have started must go on and on till it whispers against the pebbles on the farther shore. So it is with a good deed or an evil one; we see its beginning; we cannot see what distant shore it may reach. So, no one will ever know the full amount of good that this noble woman has done. The Sanitary Commission of our own Civil War, the Red Cross which to-day counts its workers by thousands in every part of the civilized world, both owed their first impulse to the pebble dropped by Florence Nightingale—even her own life, given freely to suffering humanity.

I have never seen, but I like to think of the quiet room in London, where she lies to-day in the white beauty of her age. Nearly ninety years have passed since the little girl-baby woke to life among the blossoms of the City of Flowers; more than half a century has gone by since the Lady with the Lamp passed like light along the corridors of the Barrack Hospital; yet still Florence Nightingale lives and loves, still her thoughts go out in tenderness and compassion toward all who are "in trouble, sorrow, need, sickness, or any other adversity."

Let us think of that quiet room as one of the holy places of the earth; let us think of her, and take our leave of her, with loving and thankful hearts.